DEDICATION

To my wonderful mother, Patsy,
who in the latter years of her life
became my biggest cheerleader.
I love you with all my heart!
— "Your Firstborn"

ACKNOWLEDGMENT

To my office family at Bozzuto Insurance:
Thank you for sharing your workspace with me.
Thank you for giving me a safe and beautiful place to think and write.
Your spirit of excellence is infectious and made this book possible.

Thank you to all my friends, family and colleagues who supported me.

Published by Freedom Focus, Sacramento, CA
Author Website: www.patricelynn.com

RISE TO SUCCESS™

BY PATRICE LYNN

Contents

PART 3 BEYOND SCIENCE TO THE SUPERNATURAL

PART 4 HOW TO RISE TO SUCCESS IN 15 MINUTES PER DAY

EVER WONDER IF YOU ARE USING YOUR BRAIN'S
FULL POTENTIAL TO REACH YOUR BEST RESULTS?

- Do you want more for your future, but aren't sure how to get it?
- Are you tired of traditional goal setting that never seems to work?
- Do you know more about how to program your cell phone than your brain?

**If you answered "Yes" to any of these questions,
then this book is for you!**

RISE TO SUCCESS IS THE KEY TO OVERCOME
YOUR CHALLENGES AND CREATE A SUCCESSFUL LIFE

———————————————————————

COPYRIGHT © 2018 PATRICE LYNN

RISE TO SUCCESS™
Retrain Your Brain
Recharge Your Life
Results in 15 Minutes

ISBN 978-1-7322330-0-3 *Paperback*
      978-1-7322330-1-0 *Ebook*
      978-1-7322330-2-7 *Audio book*

Illustrations by Patrice Lynn
Book cover design by Debbie O'Byrne — Jetlaunch
Author professional photo by Jessica Foster — Laced Boudoir

Published by Freedom Focus, Sacramento, CA
Autor website: www.patricelynn.com

RISE to Success — Foreword by Troy McClain

As an inspirational speaker and for life in general, I will always believe in training the brain for positive outcomes. Most of the great leaders have this in common as they are constantly practicing a system of positive belief. This is exactly why Patrice Lynn's book is a must read for anyone looking for additional light, love and powerful results in their life!

Patrice and I have known each other for some time now. Her valued information, along with a beautiful personality that shines within these pages, is only out shadowed when you meet her in person. Armed with twenty years of professional training and coaching experience, and a lifetime of study, she approaches training the mind in a simple, fun fashion. During our time together, I have found her to be insightful, authentic and real. The same rings true within these pages. The information is insightful, authentic and real.

RISE to Success will begin to exercise your brain and shape your thoughts in a way that will elevate your positive mindset and mitigate, if not do away with all together, your negative thoughts and being. As you move past this page and enter a new chapter, start your mind right by smiling — because this is the beginning of your *RISE to Success*!

Troy McClain is an international trainer of positive mindset, strategic planning and creative thinking. He has been invited to participate in the highest levels of thought leadership with the likes of Trudeau, President Trump, Buffet and more. He placed fourth in the first season of the popular television show, *The Apprentice*. Some know him as the honored and humbled leader who was asked to step up and enhance the qualities and experiences within a global success club known as "GIN". Others may have gone through his leadership training courses located in Boise, Idaho.

RISE to Success — Introduction by Patrice Lynn

Recently I started sharing with people what I know about how to get positive results utilizing neuroscience, mental imagery, spaced repetition and quantum physics. I was surprised by how curious people were and how much they wanted to incorporate these principles into their life. It was then that I realized I had touched on something powerful.

I heard a rallying cry from people who want big-time results that bring freedom, joy and true prosperity. That's when I decided to go public with my signature program, **RISE to Success**. How you think repetitively, what you imagine, the words you speak and how you feel — the **RISE**.

By sharing the brain techniques and insights in this book, I want to be your change agent. That is, you will begin to see a new reality, a new paradigm to easily unleash more of your potential with the **RISE to Success** daily system. These are things I have personally experienced on my own journey. I spent years of trial and error perfecting the process — with lessons learned and exciting results. Now you can use it as the ultimate shortcut to your success and reach your goals and dreams with renewed hope and optimism.

Do you know someone facing big personal challenges? Maybe even you? The world around us appears to be in a never-ending turbulent storm. While writing this book, natural disasters broke out around the globe. Physical and mental health challenges are at an all time high. Political unrest and racial tension threaten conventional safety and security. The pace of change has accelerated for all of us.

That is exactly why this book is so important right now. **RISE to Success** will help you to rise above the noise and find your center — the calm in the storm. The moment you react to these external events with the survival programming of the subconscious mind, you live on autopilot. You give away your power and live from a state of fear and anxiety. Because we are all connected, this negativity impacts you and everyone around you.

Whatever your brain thinks and your body feels, you will produce more of — just like your trillions of cells multiplying every day. This multiplication is great as long as you stay focused on what you *want*, instead of what you *don't want*. The brain programing I share with you through **RISE** will keep you from reacting to external events by putting your attention in the right place. Being present and aware gives you the internal ability to create a life you love in any environment.

My life is an example that anyone can overcome challenges through the personal growth methods outlined in this book. In these pages I will reveal to you what I know, and hopefully make some fascinating connections between several areas of brain science, psychology, human performance, inner healing, physics, and spirituality. With **RISE to Success** I will show you how to keep your positive "vibe" up and draw more positive to you; like bees to honey, your life will gradually taste sweeter.

How RISE to Success Came From My Own Challenges

Many of you will remember the mortgage crisis that triggered the financial collapse of 2008-2009. It was a terrible time for me not just as a business owner but personally as well. Even though the stress was intense, my intuition began to speak to me to "lighten the load" (which I did) or I would have been hit even harder.

The work I was doing at the time, coaching owners on their businesses, was the type of business expense that was the first to go.

Many entrepreneurs, myself included, lost all their clients and income. *Talk about fear and anxiety*. And to make matters worse, over a nine-month period I also experienced the death of two stepparents, a very sad relationship breakup, accident/knee surgery, and two minor car accidents. I was a mess.

For the next year and a half I found new consulting clients and kept my cash flow alive, but I had accumulated quite a bit of debt after buying a home, a car and a business franchise. This weighed heavily on me and I was not much fun to be around. Life suddenly seemed so serious and dark. By the spring of 2010, I knew I would need to sell my newly renovated 1929 Tudor home and start over.

Miraculously, I used the **RISE to Success** system to get out of debt within months of my decision, and stay on a prosperous trajectory almost a decade later. Along with my spiritual faith, **RISE to Success** became my framework for happiness and well-being.

Once I made my decision to recalibrate, the ideas came quickly to produce my desires. In 2008, John Assaraf's book, *The Answer,* seemed to jump off the shelf of an airport gift store into my hands. I read it and found the brain science and methodical daily imprinting quite fascinating. Two years later I was drawn back to the book and other experts like Jim Rohn, Bob Proctor, Laurel Langemeier and Jack Canfield who were saying some of the same things. All of a sudden it dawned on me that I could combine their wisdom into my own process that I had been refining over the years.

Throughout my twenty years in personal and professional development I had already used many of these techniques, just not in a **RISE to Success** workbook or journal format and not with a consistent, daily focus on all of the required elements. As I applied these techniques, results happened so quickly that even I was amazed.

Becoming Debt Free and Living the Dream

Not only was I able to use **RISE to Success** for financial progress since 2010, I have lived quite a life. Money and favor have seemed at times to fall out of the heavens. I have traveled extensively; I wintered in

Palm Desert, wrote much of my book in Sedona, and hiked in the Rockies for two summers.

I was incredibly blessed to be able to take off five months to work alongside my sister and help my Mom transition to assisted living after a series of strokes, falls and surgery. Being there in her time of need, and spending time in Ohio with extended family, childhood neighbors and high school friends will always be a highlight of my life. What a precious time I will cherish forever.

Since 2010, I also generated incomes in short periods by designing training on a global level, which was rewarding. I then had the time, freedom and resources to grow spiritually, as well as discover and heal from my early stage trauma patterns revealed through energy healing. The acronym for **RISE** (you'll see it below) was given to me as a pure gift from God during that restorative phase of my life. Since that revelation, I developed this signature program, wrote this book, and began to share it with others.

Recently, I moved into to a lovely home in northern California, where I am strategically positioned to reach many people with this timely message. **RISE to Success** has helped me design a rich and wonderful life. These same types of results are awaiting you, too, as you incorporate these principles day-by-day into your life.

RISE to Success is Organized in the Following Way

In **Part One:** "How to Wire All of Your Brain for Success", you will activate your conscious mind to identify exactly what you want by using REPETITION, IMAGES, SOUND, and EMOTION in smart ways (RISE). This process is where the power lies. The **RISE** design will enable you to be present, positive and mindful as you become aware of what you think, see, say and feel. Real life examples illustrate for you the strength and effectiveness of these principles.

Part Two: "Positive Results from the Inside Out", dives into the inner world of change and helps make sense of the driving forces that work for you and the restraining forces that push against you. Here you will learn how beliefs are actually formed and how to override old programs of your subconscious mind, liberating your life. You will love the insights that encourage you to let go of certain parts of outdated, traditional goal setting in favor of goals aligned to your "Sweet Spot".

Part Three: "Beyond Science to the Supernatural" explains — in simple terms — how to harness brain science, quantum physics, and spiritual dimensions that will help manifest your vision. When you imagine the future you desire, your brain perceives it as if you are experiencing it in real time, bringing reality from the future to the present moment. As you understand your brain's natural state of energy, vibration and frequency you can tap into supernatural results.

In **Part Four:** "How to Rise To Success in 15 Minutes Per Day", you will learn specifically *how* to establish an empowering 15-minute daily routine using the **RISE to Success Journal**. The world's wealthiest agree a powerful morning routine contributes to greater levels of success, expanded creativity, optimism, and inner peace. As you consistently start your day with this brain activation ritual you will feel increasingly in control of your destiny.

When you implement **RISE to Success** you will have more freedom and fulfillment. You will be able to:

- **Direct your brain with cutting edge techniques** from the field of neuroscience and use these astounding discoveries to **change your circumstances for the better**.
- **Raise your energy level and self-confidence** to feel strong, positive, and grateful each day as your motivation grows from the inside out.
- Use images to generate more results in less time, causing a **substantial expansion** in your personal and professional life.
- **Change your beliefs from lack to prosperity** and achieve clarity, focus, and specific daily strategies to **live a rich life.**
- Operate in the world system we live in, but learn to rise above stress and negativity and **use supernatural principles to call results into reality**.

As you **RISE** you will discover how to take charge and live your life as you choose. True success is living life exactly as you want; not how anyone else wants to, but doing what makes you truly happy and content. You will begin to live your best life as you apply **RISE to Success** technology — one step at a time, and one new behavior at a time.

You can download "Free Gifts" at www.patricelynn.com

The information provided in this book is designed to provide helpful information on the subjects discussed. This book is not meant to be used, nor should it be used, to diagnose or treat any medical condition. It is sold with the understanding that the author and publisher are not engaged to render any type of psychological, legal, or any other kind of professional advice. For diagnosis or treatment of any medical problem, consult your own physician. Neither the publisher nor the individual author shall be liable for any physical, psychological, emotional, financial, or commercial damages, including, but not limited to, special, incidental, consequential or other damages. References are provided for informational purposes only and do not constitute endorsement of any websites or other sources. Readers should be aware that the websites listed in this book might change.

PART 1

HOW TO WIRE ALL OF YOUR BRAIN FOR SUCCESS

Master the Four Simple Steps of RISE to Success

RISE to Success is a simple system to create positive results in your life in as little as 15 minutes a day. Success is a habit, and when you program your brain intentionally every day, you will get powerful results. For this formula to work effectively, you are encouraged to take consistent action. Otherwise, your life will likely not change. The secret of your success will be found in your daily routine.

Think of this book as a series of building blocks to help you learn the strategies, mindsets, and science that only a select few know.

Each day you will design a life you love. People, events and opportunities will come into your life as a direct result of how you **RISE**. Let's make sure they are the circumstances and events you *really* want. Interestingly, you have already been using this system, but you were not consciously aware of its power and impact. Now you will be.

Over the course of my lifetime I have used the **RISE to Success** system to experience wonderful progress. I will give you real life examples as well as the knowledge that makes this process work. You will not have to read numerous books on this subject because I have distilled the best nuggets of wisdom into this one resource. I have done the research and experimented in my

TIP
Success is about living the life that *you* want to live

own life laboratory. I learned what blocks success and what creates it. Now you can apply the **RISE** and become the person you were meant to be.

With **RISE**, you will take the steps to achieve the results that define a brilliant life path, uniquely yours.

Part One - The Foundation Of The RISE To Success System

The RISE acronym is an excellent framework by which to remember all four steps, which function synergistically to help you live your best life. Here's a quick snapshot of basic principles you will learn:

- REPETITION – Thoughts you think over and over that become automatic
- IMAGES – The sensory rich images you see in your mind's eye
- SOUND – The words you speak and the power they emit
- EMOTION – Feelings that radiate positive or negative energy

In Part One, you will activate your conscious mind to identify exactly what you want by using REPETITION, IMAGES, SOUND, and EMOTION in smart ways. This process is where the power lies. The RISE design will enable you to be present, positive and mindful each day with a beautiful morning routine.

Shape Up Physically and Mentally with Consistent Discipline

I wrote much of this book while in Sedona, Arizona. Every morning I would hike 45 minutes up Sugarloaf, one of the local mountains with stunning vistas. With this consistent, methodical effort, I strengthened my lungs and legs. Once acclimated, I was no longer breathing hard or breaking a sweat to reach the top. My body got stronger as I committed to this habit of activity.

This is exactly how a daily commitment to **RISE to Success** will help wire your brain for positive results. Each day you will recondition and build the cells in your brain so that they will link up to new thought patterns and new belief systems. With this new brain wiring, your success will happen naturally and organically — *from the inside out* — as opposed to relying on willpower to make it happen from the outside in. This is the best, and least stressful way to go.

This is not an insurmountable task. Like my morning hikes up the mountain, the steps you take every day in the **RISE** program will become increasingly easy.

Even 15 Minutes of Daily Effort Reaps Results

What's more, there is a tool to help with this morning routine. Using the **RISE to Success Journal** you simply fill in the blank sections, doable in 15 minutes a day. Of course, you can invest more time and incorporate more activities. But that is up to you. What's the attractiveness of **RISE**? You can design it your own way!

Nike's "Just Do It" slogan has resonated in our culture for years. I am confident that you share this attitude; the fact you are reading this book shows you are a special person orientated to success. I understand how fast-paced life is today, but setting aside 15 minutes daily to this ritual is possible for anyone. As a student of human behavior, I know as you focus like a laser, your results will accelerate over time. Yes, it is as simple as you *just doing it*.

Goal: Positive Ball of Energy Becomes Bigger Than the Negative Ball

Think of your life as a big ball of energy. All of your current thoughts, feelings, imaginations and actions radiate positive or negative energy. All of your past beliefs, subconscious programming, stored images, and cellular memories emit positive or negative energy. The combination adds up to a measurable level. Whether you radiate more positive or negative energy is a combination of many things, many of which you may not be aware. Whether you are aware or not, your ball of energy still impacts your results. This drawing illustrates the dynamic:

YOUR ENERGY

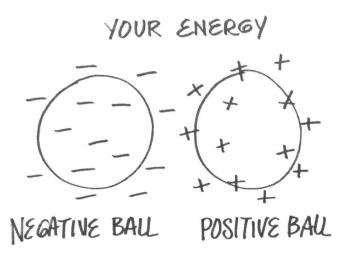

NEGATIVE BALL   POSITIVE BALL

Now, imagine your positive ball of energy becoming bigger than your negative ball. What will it take to make this happen? What activities will release this kind of power? Following are the main ones to build the positive side:

1. Programming the brain daily; thoughts, feelings, images, words
2. Listening to audio programs
3. Reading inspirational books
4. Building relationships with success-minded people
5. Exercise, nutrition and wellness
6. Spiritual practices

The more you do these actions, the more you emphasize and feed the positive. The timing is different for everyone, but one day you realize your positive ball of energy is greater than your negative. I knew a man, Phil, who said it happened for him in about five months of focused intention. As you can probably guess, **RISE to Success** is designed to help make this expansion happen.

Imagine what is possible for you when you are emanating positive energy everywhere you go. What would it feel like to have the negative ball shrivel up because you are not giving it any attention or feeding it with negative thoughts? When your positive ball is bigger, what kind of opportunities will come your way? Who might be attracted to you? What doors will open? What events will transpire? It's fun to think of the prospects this will bring, isn't it?

The goal of our work together with **RISE** is definitely for your positive ball of energy to become bigger than your negative ball. Take in this simple, but immensely powerful visual image:

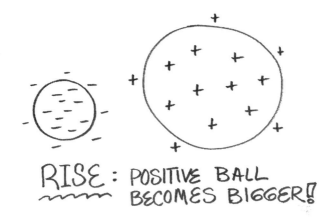

RISE : POSITIVE BALL BECOMES BIGGER!

The Brain is The Ultimate User Interface

Mysterious, methodical, and magnificent, the brain plays a leading role in your **RISE to Success**. Your brain will be a powerful ally in your quest to build a positive ball of energy. Let's compare the brain to the cellphone to understand its intrinsic capabilities.

Technology has accelerated so rapidly that it's easy to take for granted the tool we each hold in our hands every day: the cellphone — astonishing in its processing speed and ability. We rely on these devices to text, email, talk, map routes, research, share photos and videos, and review and recommend products and services. Most importantly, our cell phones connect us to those we know and love and those we have never met, including colleagues and business partners on the other side of the world.

Operating these mini computers is user-friendly, thanks to the intuitive interface designed by brilliant minds in the technology sector. However, in comparison to the cell phone, *our brain is infinitely more powerful*. This magnificent three-pound organ sits above your neck. Yet we know very little about how to program our own super computer to get the results we want in our lives. **RISE to Success** is designed to change all that. Now is the time to shift your paradigm and learn how and why your brain, not a computer, is the ultimate user interface.

Visual Flowchart: From Paradigms and Beliefs to Results

Throughout my career as a life coach and trainer, I have learned that results in life flow in a predictable pattern. This diagram illustrates a flowchart of these stages:

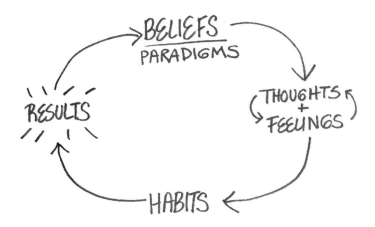

Paradigm Shifts Change Your Map Of Reality

Achieving results in life starts with your view of reality — that is, your paradigm. Although the term dates from the 1700s, Stephen R. Covey popularized it in the 1990s in his book *The 7 Habits of Highly Effective People*. Many people, especially in business, talked about the merits of "paradigm shifting".

Let's boil down the meaning of this term. A "paradigm shift" is a fundamental change in your view of reality based on new, revolutionary information or ideas.

For example, more than 10,000 years ago the agricultural revolution precipitated a paradigm shift from hunting and gathering food to growing it in a field. Farms naturally led to the founding of towns and cities. People once commonly believed that the world was flat and that the sun revolved around the earth. However, in the 1600s, astronomer Galileo reinforced Copernicus' ancient theory that all planets revolve around the sun. Although Galileo was imprisoned for his belief, it gained acceptance by scientists and other educated individuals.

Our first voyage to the moon in 1969 shifted the entire world's view of what's possible and launched us into further space exploration. In my lifetime, the Internet and personal computing led the shift from the industrial age to the information age. Usually people who are agents of change with new insights inspire paradigm shifts. They help us to see truth a bit differently. Because of them our minds become open to new ways of operating in life.

Wiring your brain for positive results in the way outlined in this book could be a new paradigm for you. As you embrace this new way of living life, you are one step closer to the life you want.

BELIEFS Determine Our Health, Wealth, and Happiness in Life

Standing alongside paradigms are our beliefs: a term used often in recent years. One day its true origin was revealed to me, and I realized that the formation of beliefs is simpler and more straightforward than previously imagined. Beliefs can be shaped internally by you or externally by other people in your environment: parents, teachers, friends, family, and social media. We will delve into both aspects of beliefs much deeper in Part Two.

Rosie is a joy-filled person who has the following internal beliefs:

- Life is full of adventure.
- I am a loving, kind and creative person.
- My life is valuable.
- I deserve good things and to be happy.

Ralph is a first-class worrier who has some limiting beliefs inside of him:

- Everything must be perfect in life.
- If I don't tell people what to do, nothing will get done right.
- My past actions were shameful and despicable.
- I don't really trust others or myself.

Beliefs do shape your reality because they drive your behavior. You can, however identify and then change your beliefs. This will happen each day as you think, see, say, and feel what you want in your **RISE to**

Success Journal. You will program and reprogram your belief system, relieve anxiety as you refocus your mind, and build a solid foundation of success and wellbeing.

RISE to Success Journal: You can download a *free copy* of the daily form to make your own journal under "Free Gifts" at www.patrice-lynn.com. You can also order a pre-made journal and **RISE to Success Journal** Mini Course under "Products" at www.patricelynn.com.

THOUGHTS and FEELINGS Create a Feedback Loop That Leads to Results

Did you know that every time you have a thought, your brain releases a chemical? Positive thoughts produce upper brain chemicals such as dopamine, the "feel good" chemical. Negative thoughts produce downer brain chemicals such as cortisol, the "stress" chemical. These chemicals affect your moods. The way you think and feel can range from happy, positive, joyful, and grateful to upset, angry, unworthy, and fearful.

As you can see, this process can become a vicious cycle towards negative results or an uplifting cycle towards positive results. Over time, it becomes easy to repeat some of the same thoughts and feelings over and over.

Once you understand this mind-body connection you can harness your thoughts and associated feelings in the direction you desire. Here's the good news: you have a lot more control over this than you may believe. By sharing what I have learned and experienced, I want to empower you to take charge of *what you think* and *how you feel* so that the positive overrides the negative on a consistent basis. And your positive ball grows bigger.

TIP
Consistent positive thoughts override negative ones

New Success HABITS Will Become Automatic Programs

Practicing **RISE** over and over until it becomes a habit triggers your brain's automatic mechanism, your subconscious mind. As you consistently take action you will develop new success habits. When you replace those old ways of being/doing (that no longer serve you) with those that do, your brain will remember them for future use. Now trained to respond, the automatic mechanism repeats successful actions as habits.

Those professionals who have practiced and automated their trade or skills provide great examples for success-habits. Top-performing sales professionals respond to objections or concerns without missing a beat; they are conditioned to offer the right response at the right time. Successful sports figures and high achievers in all fields have habits that become second nature, indeed instinctual, through repetition.

Like these successful individuals, you, too, can produce the life you're impassioned to live. As you program your brain, you will be inspired to take action and make your desire a reality. The inspired actions you take will lead to results.

How Will You Accomplish These Results?

Using the **RISE to Success** program, you will identify what you want in the following way:

Clear Intention + High Vibe Emotion = Tangible Results

Defined by *Wikipedia*, "Intention represents a mental state that expresses a commitment to carrying out an action or actions in the future". When you match your intention with an elevated emotion of what it will feel like to live out the intention, you set up the natural laws of attraction. People, events, and opportunities will move toward you in a manner that may surprise you. Not every time do results happen quickly and magically, but they can. You literally affect physical matter with your mind, which becomes the fun part of the game of life. You begin to achieve the positive, tangible results you want.

RESULTS *You Choose* Are The Ultimate Desired Outcome

It's up to you to choose the outcomes that are custom designed for you. Results flow from your paradigms and beliefs, thoughts and feelings — all reinforced by the daily rituals you practice and the *actions* you execute. Each day you design a life you love.

The **RISE to Success** system will guide you to the results you want. What will they be?

- Having dinner with your family every night?
- Climbing a 14,000-foot mountain?
- Building a $2 million investment account?
- Learning to play the guitar?
- Driving the sports car of your dreams?
- Traveling the world?
- Giving $10,000 annually to a charitable cause close to your heart?
- Adopting children from a different country?
- Remodeling your backyard with an outdoor kitchen?

Walt Disney's Story: Dream the Dream, then Hold Until You "See It"

Everyone in America has either been to or knows about *Disneyland* and *Disney World*. One of my favorite stories is about Walt Disney and his ability to utilize his own **RISE to Success** principles to create these magical kingdoms.

Walt's first wonderful creation was *Disneyland*, a theme park that opened in Anaheim, California in 1955. Not long after, he began to envision a much larger property unencumbered by a big city like Los Angeles, so he secretly began buying land in Florida from 1959 until 1966, the year he died. His brother Roy Disney, who had been Walt's partner since the earliest production of Disney cartoon days in the 1920s, took over construction of the *Walt Disney World* project.

Julie Andrews gave a live performance on the opening day at *Disney World* in 1971, and Roy O. Disney dedicated the new theme park to his brother, Walt.

A plaque near the entrance reads:

"Walt Disney World is a tribute to the philosophy and life of Walter Elias Disney . . . and to the talents, the dedication, and the loyalty of the entire Disney organization that made Walt Disney's dream come true. May Walt Disney World bring Joy and Inspiration and New Knowledge to all who come to this happy place . . . a Magic Kingdom where the young at heart of all ages can laugh and play and learn — together. Dedicated this 25th day of October, 1971."

Roy Oliver Disney

At the dedication, a businessman turned to Roy and exclaimed; "It is too bad Walt couldn't have lived to see this."

Surprised, Roy turned to him and simply said, "*He did see it*. That is why it is here."

That one statement has inspired me throughout my life. Walt Disney did see it — thousands of times in his mind — on his personal IMAGE screen: a sensually rich vision of thousands of people, young and old, smiling, exploring, and enjoying this new kingdom he created in his mind.

We must *see it* in our mind first before our dreams can become real, even if the real, tangible part happens after we depart, like Disney. We can leave a legacy through our contributions while here on earth.

Walt Disney Practiced the RISE to Success System by:

- Thinking about his dream over and over — REPETITION
- Seeing it in his mind's eye before it was built — IMAGES
- Speaking about it to his inner circle daily — SOUND
- Feeling positive about creating a happy place — EMOTION

What is the vision in your heart that calls to you? Walt Disney was a creative genius, yet you have the same brain potential! Popular culture has long stated we only use 10 percent of our brain capacity.

While proven to be inaccurate, we may still wonder at times what hidden potential of our brain is still untapped? Walt Disney was told in grade school he was not creative, but he didn't let that opinion from his outside environment turn into a limiting belief.

Disney knew what he wanted, and he put all the principles of the **RISE** system into effect day after day until he produced the positive results he dreamed about. He didn't just dream; he spoke it, wrote it, and commanded it into reality. And you can, too.

WHAT YOU LEARNED IN CHAPTER 1:
Master the Four Simple Steps of RISE to Success

From this day forward, you can use **RISE to Success** to program your brain for positive change. Fifteen minutes of daily discipline will create results. This is your golden ticket to get results *better – faster – cheaper* than ever before.

- Now you can access new brain technology to achieve your goals and dreams. Your brain is much more powerful than a cell phone mini computer.
- You can accomplish anything you want when programmed for it.
- Goal: Your positive ball of energy becomes bigger than your negative ball.
- Your life is a progression of the following:

  1. Paradigms and Beliefs
  2. Thoughts and Feelings
  3. Habits
  4. Results

- Daily practice and daily discipline generate new habits.
- You can electrically engineer your brain to create exactly the future you want to experience. Life is only as fantastic as your brain wiring makes it.
- Morning rehearsal will activate the circuits of who you want to become.

REPETITION: You Become What You Think About 2

What if you had a secret combination to open the door to the person you want to become? That code is your thoughts. Thoughts are like electric sparks that ignite your words, feelings, vision, and behaviors.

You become in your life what you think about. To empower your life, think powerful, positive, purposeful, passionate thoughts. Your thoughts will create an atmosphere around you that will throw you into a ditch or catapult you to the mountaintop. You decide!

The **RISE to Success** system begins with REPETITION.

Did you know that we have about 60,000 thoughts per day, but the trouble is that 95 percent are the same ones we had yesterday? Here's a sobering thought: even if you want your life to take a new direction but choose to retain habitual thoughts, you will go nowhere. In effect, you will remain stuck with the typical results your repetitive thoughts create.

> **TIP**
> The thoughts you think the most are the easiest ones to think

You Have Shaped Everything in Your Life with Your Thinking

Once you realize your own thoughts have created everything in your life, does that motivate you to think more deeply, more clearly, and more intentionally for something better? I hope so! Did anyone train us to pay attention to what we think? Parents? Teachers? Neighbors? In most cases, no — mine certainly didn't.

Throughout my career I strategically studied great thought leaders. Along the way the truth about thoughts surfaced and was imbedded into my heart and mind. Taking thoughts captive by our own volition and directing them properly is an ongoing process.

Andrew Carnegie commissioned a famous self-help book researched and written by Napoleon Hill: *Think and Grow Rich*. The book is not called *Work Hard and Grow Rich*; instead, the title incorporates the word "think" for a reason. In the late 1930s, Hill studied the wealthiest people. He discovered that the *way* they thought and *what* they thought about were paramount to their success. He discovered that thinking is even more important than working! In actuality, thinking *is* the hardest work.

"If you think you can or you think you can't, you are probably right. It is the thinking that makes it so." — Henry Ford

---

The Frontal Lobe of the Brain Generates Your Thoughts

The frontal lobe is the largest part of the brain (located behind the forehead) where the most advanced thinking takes place. Think of the frontal lobe as the CEO of your life. The CEO sits in the corner office to set a vision, make decisions, analyze, learn, concentrate, and observe.

TIP
Whatever you think about is what comes about

The CEO is an advanced thinker. The frontal lobe, also called the neocortex, is the most active segment of the brain and connects to the rest of the brain. Your conscious mind operates here, so let's make sure you use it to your best advantage to design an incredible life.

Are You Clear About What You Really Want?

Amazingly enough, most people are clearer about what they *don't want* than they are about what they *do want*. Without directing their focus and power, our thoughts resemble leaves tossed about in the wind. Does this sound like you?

Once you are clear and focused on what you really want, heaven and earth will move to bring that reality to you as quickly as possible. In Part Four, where you apply **RISE to Success**, certain activities will help you gain clarity about what you really want.

Use REPETITION to achieve high-level results in your business:

- Earn specific incomes
- Attract clients
- Secure contracts
- Complete projects
- Build an in-demand brand
- Develop high-caliber teams

Use REPETITION to achieve desired results in your personal life:

- Live a passionate life
- Attract abundance
- Establish lifelong friends
- Travel to adventurous places
- Improve your health
- Be mindful and present
- Tackle your to-do list

If you are spinning your wheels and unhappy about your current results, then REPETITION is the key to programming your subconscious mind — and establishing the powerful internal brain wiring connections to bring about your

TIP
Repetition is the key to becoming the person you want to be

heart's desires. The buried treasure lies in repeating these thoughts consistently because *your reality* will become what you think about most of the time!

Let's return to the notion that humans process about 60,000 thoughts per day. There is no hard science on this because it is tough to quantify what a thought really is. However, given the discussion in the scientific community, some experts suggest this number may be too low. If you include every electrical impulse between brain cells that stimulate a biological process (look for more on this topic in Chapter 12: "How Neuroscience Programs Your Human Computer") the number increases exponentially. Think of the possibilities if we marshal thousands of thoughts in the right direction — towards our dreams.

The Power of Focus in a Porsche in Montana

Have you ever lived in a state where there was *no speed limit*? I did. When you are young and love to drive fast, Montana in the 1990's was the place to be! My boyfriend at the time lent me his gorgeous, high performance Porsche 911 for a business meeting I had ninety miles away. With a big smile on my face, and the car wrapped around me, I executed the trek in forty-five minutes. You do the math. That's right — my average speed was 120 MPH.

To average 120 MPH for that long, I had to sustain the most intense, clear focus *on where I wanted to go*. The conditions were perfect with clear, dry roads, high sunshine, and very few people on the I-90 thoroughfare because it was past tourist season. The only potential obstacle was the other people who might have been oblivious to my presence because I was going twice as fast as they were. If they pulled out in front of me to pass another car, it could have been dangerous. Therefore, I prolonged a laser focus quite a distance ahead of me to anticipate everyone's move as I blazed by in a whir.

My life and the safety of those around me were at stake. I was confident of the car and my driving ability. But the focus was on the whole picture as it unfolded second by second and all the sensual input I had to gather to maneuver the course with success. What I felt was the exhilaration and power surge of focus at such a high level while driving *extremely fast*. This was truly a magical mountaintop experience for me.

To attain the results you want in your life will take periods of laser focus mixed with crystal clarity. As you practice you will become more and more skilled. My Porsche adventure taught me a lot about what's possible and how to hone this technique.

TIP
To Get What You Want in Life Requires Intense Focus

Let's take charge of our thought processes and think most of the time intensely and powerfully about successful outcomes in our business and personal lives. It's all about conjuring up enough passion and persistence to ingrain new patterns into your subconscious mind and letting the brain work behind the scenes for you. I always enjoy sharing the fun story about directing my thoughts to find the ideal house in four days:

Using RISE to Success to Manifest the House of Our Dreams

When my husband and I met in our twenties, we had boundless energy and drive. We decided to move in together after just a few months of dating, partly because we had known each other for many years throughout our college days in Montana. We started looking around for places to rent and happened upon a house that was for sale but needed lots of TLC. The economy was down, so the

continued

house had been on the market for a couple years. If we cleaned up the place, the owner agreed to let us move in with one month of free rent.

We scrubbed dirty ovens and floors, cleaned dusty walls, cut down knee-high grass, and unearthed beautiful flowerbeds. It was a labor of love, and we were so proud of our effort to make the place livable and enjoyable again. It was not long before passersby noticed our efforts. The once undesirable property was now quite lovely. Before our second month began (when our first rent was due), the owner informed us to wait on payment, as a buyer had indicated interest in the house.

Three weeks later, we learned about an offer on the house. Our landlord kindly told us not to pay any rent for that month or the next because our home improvements had sold the house for him. For a young couple starting out in life, three free months of rent proved a financial boon. Now we faced the task of finding a new place to live . . .

A Bright Idea Arrives — Let's Dream Big and Buy a House Together

Contemplating our situation one day, I proposed that we buy a house together. Why not? Although I had no savings and a sparse income selling western art, I believed in my heart that we could manifest the house of our dreams. I approached my partner about the idea, and he happily informed me he had some savings — enough for a down payment. I was *thrilled*. We agreed to "go for it" and forged ahead to with our new VISION.

Envisioning an outcome in this manner was not a new process for me. In fact, at the promptings of Lee Poole, my boss at The Hole in the Wall Gallery, I had previously enrolled in a personal development class called "The YES Course." The teachers, Ivan and Dagney Burnell, taught us that whatever we wanted — whether a life partner or a house — we needed to make a crystal-clear list of the ideal qualities we desired. I took this to heart and made a list describing my ideal mate. Dave, the perfect match to my list, appeared in my life.

In a depressed economy, buying a house and getting a good deal were certainly doable. Dave and I made a detailed list of what we wanted in our ideal home.

With my burgeoning interest in personal growth, I had just read the aforementioned book *Think and Grow Rich.* I followed the instruction not only to identify the list of qualities but also to close my eyes and *see* and *feel* and *believe* myself already in possession of what I wanted. I decided to give this a chance. It was the day of a good friend's wedding, and before we left to attend, I lay down on the bed, closed my eyes, and began the prescribed process in a deliberate fashion.

Imagining and Feeling the House as a Concrete Reality

One by one, I went through the items on the list and saw how Dave and I were enjoying each room, each item, and each quality. The IMAGES were sensually rich and vibrant. I also intentionally felt the EMOTION that went along with the IMAGES. My imagination ran free as I pictured entertaining guests, having a workspace to create, and relaxing outside with a view of the mountains. My heart came alive as I envisioned us together, enjoying this lifestyle. Time seemed to stand still as I went very deep within and brought the house to life on an imaginary screen in my mind.

What was the most astounding part of this story? *Four days later we were standing in the house.*

We made an appointment to see a realtor Dave knew. She could not show the house on that day, but she provided the address so we could drive by and view the property.

With the list of ideal house qualities in hand; we headed immediately into a newer

continued

Neighborhood we had never seen before on the south side of town. We loved the rural feel, with each home relatively new and situated on lots at least an acre. Suddenly, we spotted a different house than the one we were directed to, with a "For Sale by Owner" sign staked in the yard. I noticed the owners working in the garage and suggested to Dave that we just drop in.

"Really?" he said.

"Yes!" I emphatically replied.

Upon meeting the couple, we expressed interest in the house. They perked up and invited us in to see their newly built ranch home, handcrafted by the two of them. It was *gorgeous*. Details included knotty-pine vaulted ceilings in the great room with matching wainscoting on the walls, three bedrooms, two full baths, a large kitchen, an oversized garage with workbench, and a laundry area. The home sat on 1.5 acres graced by a creek in the backyard and views of three mountain ranges. We could gaze at these mountains directly from the covered front porch as well as the living room. Wow — did we hit the jackpot.

The More Connected You Are to Your Vision, The Easier It Is to See

The owners provided a summary sheet with all the features, a picture, and the sales price. We expressed interest and promised to get in touch. As we headed out in Dave's truck, I took out the list I had made, scanned it, and promptly said, "Dave, *this is the house*."

"Really?" he replied.

"Yes, it has *everything* on the list except for a sink in the garage and phone jacks in every room." I exclaimed, "This is our house!" I knew it instantly; Dave just needed a bit of time to catch up to the idea.

Because I had imprinted the list of qualities with IMAGES and tangible EMOTIONS of the home we desired deep inside me, I was the one who recognized it was "The House." After all, I had imagined this place in my mind and heart first. Therefore, it was easy for me to recognize every quality when I saw it in reality. Even though Dave was right beside me, he did not recognize it. This moment exemplified the definition of success — when "opportunity meets preparation."

If you're willing to do the work of thinking and dreaming and imagining, you will be able to recognize the events and circumstances and opportunities as they arrive on the scene. However, if you do not take the deep dive to create from within, you might be blind to the opportunity — even if it's right in front of you.

Two Happy Endings . . .

We met with the owners the next day and made an offer. It was lower than the asking price. We showed them our list and said the house had everything except the sink in the garage and the phone jacks in every room. They came back with a price in the middle and said they would put a sink in the garage and phone jacks in every room. The power of clarity to identify exactly what you want *works*.

Remember the other house that we helped sell by improving it? We had 30 days to move out. Many people told us it was *impossible* to find and buy a house in 30 days. Really? Exactly 30 days from the day we decided to buy a house and made our wish list, we located the home, obtained financing, closed on the house, and moved in! The power of REPETITION to direct our thoughts did not let us down. We conceived, believed, and achieved. Dave and I lived in the house many years and loved every minute of our Montana mountain sanctuary.

RISE to Success asks us to create our future by thinking repetitively and imagining vividly the qualities we want to experience. As we focus on what is ideal, we draw that reality to us. One of my favorite ancient sayings is, "Finally, whatever is true, whatever is honorable, whatever is just, whatever is pure, whatever is lovely, whatever is commendable, if there is any excellence, if there is anything worthy of praise, let your mind dwell on these things."

TIP
The best way to predict your future is to create it

Four Stages To Success Habits That Are Second Nature

How do you learn to develop a new skill such as REPETITION of your thoughts to bring about the results you want in life? Interestingly, the more you practice being mindful or conscious about what you want, the more capable you become at the mental process.

Something as simple as focused concentration is a skill just as golf and tennis are — activities that require regular practice.

Whenever you want to learn a new skill, you will go through the following stages — every time, no exceptions — whether it is mastering a second language, a software application, learning the tango, or implementing **RISE to Success**. The "Four Stages for Learning Any New Skill" was a theory developed at *Gordon Training International* in California by Noel Burch in the 1970's.

1. Unconscious incompetence
2. Conscious incompetence
3. Conscious competence
4. Unconscious competence

Let's use a simple, practical example of shoe tying to illustrate how you learn a new skill:

Unconscious incompetence: When you were an infant, you did not know you would one day need to learn to tie your shoes. You were clueless that you did not have the shoe tying skill. Essentially, you did not know what you did not know.

Conscious incompetence: One day you grew up and noticed your big brother was tying his shoes, but your mom was tying yours. You wanted to be like your big brother, so you tried to tie your own shoes, but you failed. You could not figure out how to accomplish this complex task. You became consciously aware that you lacked this skill.

Conscious competence: With massive trial and error and teaching from your mother and your brother, you practiced over and over to learn how to tie your own shoes. You really wanted to learn this, so you persevered and *one day you did it*. Through conscious effort and focused concentration, you became capable of tying your own shoes. With REPETITION, it became easier and easier, and with time, you graduated to the next level of learning.

Unconscious competence: When it became time to play outdoors, your brother called, "Let's go; hurry up!" By then, you put on and tied your shoes while your thoughts focused on your friends outside and where to find your baseball and glove. Over time, this skill had become automatic; a learned habit that did not require focused awareness.

When you learned to ride a bike, drive a car, and read a book, you likely were "wobbly" and needed assistance. With time and practice, you mastered the skill. Repetition at the conscious competence level ultimately leads to unconscious competence of habits.

To live the life of your dreams, unconscious competence of success habits is imperative. The best way is to set up a simple learning system that will imprint what you want from your conscious to your unconscious mind. Focus on your ideal vision over and over with **RISE to Success**.

Practice REPETITION of Success Habits by:

- Writing down goals you want in your life.
- Imagining the vision that you want.

- Speaking positive statements out loud.
- Generating positive emotion through a gratitude process.

(Look for reinforcing activities in the **RISE to Success Journal** explained in Part Four)

In conclusion, there are only two ways to reach the level of **unconscious competence**:

1 – REPETITION of the skill over and over until it becomes an ingrained pathway in your brain. At this point it is internalized and becomes a *knowing* inside of you.

2 –Observe a mentor who has accomplished the skill you want to have. Just as you learned to tie your shoes by observing your big brother, choose to listen, watch, and model your behavior after people who are masters at the skills you want to possess. Even books and videos allow us to access the mindset, knowledge and insights of experts. Many leaders are readers and have been mentored by people they met through the soulful pages of a book or online program.

It takes brainpower, focus, attention, concentration — *it is work*. And yet, the payoff is great when our thoughts are organized and aligned with what we want. Thoughts are things. What we think creates our reality. Let's get to work and do this right. Thinking is hard work and the payoff is magnificent.

Here is a quick review so far of how you will **RISE to Success**:

1. Use REPETITION to think over and over about what you want. Write these goals down in the journal to imprint them daily into your brain.

What You Learned in Chapter 2:
REPETITION: You Become What You Think About

Use the **RISE to Success** system to wire your brain for positive results. Pay attention to what you want, making it a magnificent obsession.

That requires directing your thoughts on purpose. Bottom line: we can develop this skill with practice through REPETITION and mental rehearsal. We can focus our thoughts on something we have not yet created. If properly wired, we can achieve what we desire.

- Our thoughts create *everything* that happens to us. So, if you can change your thoughts, you can change your results, and rethink yourself into the life you've always imagined for yourself.
- Thoughts are the electric sparks that ignite your words, feelings, vision, and behaviors.
- REPETITION of what you think, feel, see, say, and do will bring about definite results. Make sure they are the results you *want*, not the ones you *don't want*.
- Don't get pulled into a negative vortex of despair, anxiety, and victim mentality; **RISE** above and redesign your thoughts to drive where you want to go in life.
- Thoughts start off as *conscious* and then become *unconscious* — that is, automatic thought programs, or *habits*.

3 IMAGES: Bring Vision into Reality on Your "Image-screen"

"Imagination is more important than knowledge. For knowledge is limited to all we now know and understand, while imagination embraces the entire world, and all there ever will be to know and understand." — Albert Einstein

Have you ever wondered what exists beyond the world as you see it from your physical eyes? From the most distant stars to the inner landscape of our cells, there are internal and external mechanisms that exist beyond our physical senses.

As the story goes, Albert Einstein discovered the theory of relativity daydreaming on a grassy hillside while gazing at the clouds. Just like a photograph that appears on blank paper when placed in a tray of chemicals, we can be a catalyst to bring vision into tangible reality through visual IMAGES.

In the second step of **RISE to Success**, we will explore how IMAGES, imagination, mental rehearsal, and sensory-rich visualization will activate the physical laws of nature to bring you positive results. Your mind holds an "Image-screen" — like a TV, computer, or phone screen that you can learn to operate. On this screen, you can use your imagination to create a positive mental movie of your ideal future. On this screen, you can also erase negative memory pictures and override them with new programs of joy, happiness, and well being.

We started **RISE** with REPETITION, the step that affects all the other steps. As you start each day repeating an internal vision of your ideal future, you will imprint these glorious IMAGES into your subconscious mind, belief system, and brain.

Here's the kicker: your brain does not easily differentiate between what you see in your current life with your own two eyes, and those clear, powerful, positive images you feed it. You have been given the capacity to imagine something and transform it into reality. What's the catch? *You must make the choice to use it.*

"Your time is limited, so don't waste it living someone else's life." — Steve Jobs, Apple

---

Many heartwarming stories and examples illustrate how this works. Once you learn and apply fun and creative imaging techniques, your view of reality, paradigms, and beliefs will never be the same. Along the way, you'll discover more capability than you ever dreamed possible. J.K. Rowling, the famous Harry Potter author and the world's first self-made billionaire author, offers an inspiring observation: "We do not need *magic* to change the world, we carry all the power we need inside ourselves already: *we have the power to imagine better*." How well are you using this power every day? Let's jumpstart IMAGES.

TIP
Imagination is the birthplace of human improvement

How Familiar Are You with Activating IMAGES?

Throughout my life I have known the power of IMAGES rich with details. Here are several that resonate today:

- Picturing Daddy's car pulling into the driveway.
- Anticipating joy and surprise at family Easter egg hunts.

- Awaiting a new love note from my boyfriend.
- Visualizing my discharge from the hospital to attend senior prom.
- Envisioning our first house as we wanted it to be
- Imagining success as a speaker.
- Seeing myself hike with a celebrity.

VISUAL

Anyone Can Learn to Visualize with Practice

As a learning specialist, I discovered 70 percent of people are visual learners. If you are not one, you can learn to leverage this power. It is possible to heighten your ability to visualize when you practice daily. Right now, close your eyes and imagine a party with close friends, filled with laughter, delicious food, candlelight and hugs and smiles. How did you do? Could you see it? Did you create a vision on your internal "Image-screen" with specific details? This ability is a skill you are able to develop and grow.

Interested in other ways to imagine a positive future? Use props, such as pictures from magazines and photos online. Go to a jewelry shop, car dealer, or home improvement store and look around; touch, see and smell the objects you desire.

Consistently zero in on what you want. Focus and it will become a reality. Here's a brain hack: ask someone to snap a picture of you with the very thing you want. Keep looking at that image. In Part Four, you will learn more of these simple brain trick techniques in detail. Next is a fun example of just this sort of experience:

My Tesla Experience: An Instant Manifestation

When I was traveling quite a bit around the country, I drove a Dodge van with generous storage space for all my professional props and gear. One day my mind wandered to thoughts of owning another SUV, however I wasn't sure which one I wanted. Immediately after that thought, I drove into a full-service car wash. After finishing my conversation with the service team, I noticed an unusual SUV with an unrecognizable logo on the front.

With the owner standing nearby, I said, "What kind of car is that?"

He responded with the pride of a new dad, "It's a Tesla!" Aha. I had heard about the new Tesla SUV but had never seen one.

Eager to tell me about his new Tesla, the owner pointed out its wonderful features: batteries placed underneath which stabilized the ride, the roll bar in the front (which practically ensures no one will be injured in an accident), and the falcon wing doors to access the roomy back seats.

Then he said, "You have to sit in it to experience the best part." Happy to oblige, I crawled into the front seat and was immediately drawn to the rich tawny brown color, the quality of the leather, the smell, the feel, and the craftsmanship. I felt encapsulated by luxury.

The owner also pointed out the mass of glass that went from the base of the windshield to the middle of the vehicle.

"Wow" I exclaimed, "I have never seen anything like this." What a striking panoramic view. I felt as if I were seated in a gondola, not a car.

Put Yourself in the Picture When You "Dream Build"

While holding the gorgeous leather steering wheel and taking in the magic of this exquisite new car moment, the thought occurred to me

continued

to capture a picture. (Remember: it's always best to see yourself in the picture. If an actual photo is not possible, use photo edit tools to create one). I asked the owner to take my picture as I bonded with the experience and began to imagine it as mine.

The owner was incredibly cooperative as he took several photos with my cellphone. But what truly warmed my heart was his comment: "I do this kind of thing all the time."

"Of course, you do" I exclaimed. I knew in my heart that is why he is the proud owner of a state-of-the-art, fully electric, navy blue Tesla SUV Model X.

I walked away with a huge smile on my face and a picture of me behind the wheel of a Tesla in my phone. *I felt fantastic*. What a magical moment that was — totally unplanned, unscripted, unexpected — just the way the quantum field can deliver it to us when we are open and receptive. (Does the ending of that sentence surprise you? You'll learn more about this concept in Chapter 13: "Quantum Physics Doesn't Have to Be Hard — Here's Why").

A big smile crossed my face about the synchronicity of it all. My mind focused on what I had attracted only minutes after I had been future-dreaming about my next SUV. Well, maybe I will decide to have a Tesla SUV one day. After all, I got the picture!

IMAGES Go Beyond Just Seeing with the Eyes — They Train Your Brain

New brain-scanning technology shows that conscious perception activates the same brain areas as imagination. With imagination you do not just think about a hoped-for goal; you *visualize* it with tremendous intensity, using all your senses. This releases powerful internal forces to bring astonishing results into your life, attracting the victories and richness your heart desires. Whatever your current circumstances in business, cash flow, relationships, or health, you can

TIP
Think from your future instead of your past

drastically improve them and even create what you want them to be by using IMAGES, vision, and imagination.

Do you lack energy, clients, money, happiness or empowering beliefs? Do you think constantly about the things you lack? Do you focus your imagination on this lack to the point that it engulfs your life? Do you see those IMAGES over and over? It's time to banish those thoughts and replace them with IMAGES of prosperity, abundance, flow, and other positive results you really want. Thoughts and images stick around when we habitually think them through REPETITION.

In Chapter 1: "Master the Four Simple Steps of RISE to Success", we learned how habits are formed, and how you become what you think, feel, and do over and over. Let's repeat an essential ingredient to the **RISE** system: The repetition of IMAGES you select to create your future.

If you cannot see yourself doing it on your Image-screen, then you won't do it. This explains the failures, frustrations, and confusions of our life. We know what we want intellectually, but we can't do it because the mind cannot see it happening. When the Image-screen sees what you want clearly on the inside first, then the action can happen on the outside.

World Champion golfer Jack Nicklaus illustrates this point well. Nicklaus said: "I never hit a shot, not even in practice, without having a very sharp in-focus picture of it in my head". Turns out a lot of high performing athletes do similar mental rehearsals.

In the **RISE to Success Journal** (Part Four), you will learn in detail exactly how to create these mental movies with IMAGES of your ideal life. For now, I offer four tips to make the magic work for you:

1. Define your vision every day in sensually rich detail.
2. Play the mind movie on your Image-screen for one to two minutes.
3. Hold your focus on this and nothing else.
4. Gradually increase the frequency, duration, and intensity of your movie.

> "Imaging is positive thinking carried one step further."
> — Norman Vincent Peale, *The Power of Positive Imaging*

If you are like me, it really helps to see some examples. Let's look at three different scenarios of people who used REPETITION of visual IMAGES to create success in finances, love relationships, health, and athletic championships.

A Peak Performance Expert IMAGES His Goals

As a young man, Tony Robbins would repeat statements out loud to stay focused on his goals while running. His statements are what I call "declarations" in the SOUND part of **RISE to Success**. He believed that to achieve success in both finances and life, envisioning one's goals was crucial. He used IMAGES to create the life he wanted.

In a video on his website, Robbins says, "I would envision God's wealth circulating my life, and I would see the wealth of love, friendship, and impact, and growth, and economics . . . I'd see this wealth of abundance flowing, oceans of it, into my life."

Robbins created a metaphor for the flow of the prosperity and riches he wanted by using the power and intensity of the ocean. No wonder he owns over a hundred businesses and is worth mega millions of dollars. Tony also says, "People who fail focus on what they will have to go through; people who succeed focus on what it will feel like at the end."

A Cancer Victim Lights Up His Brain with IMAGES of Cellular Battle

James received a cancer diagnosis. He became cancer free by imaging up to 100 times per day an army of white blood cells cascading through his body, sweeping through his veins, attacking the malignant cells, and destroying them. He replayed these scenarios day after day. Replaying the battle scene in his mind especially made him feel *terrific*. This is how you, too, can **RISE to Success**: Use creative visualization to see IMAGES and feel the EMOTION. After a while and with consistent practice, the IMAGES can become just as clear as if coming through a computer or TV screen.

An Olympian Uses IMAGES of the Medal Ceremony Daily to Secure Victory

Long before Bruce Jenner became Caitlin Jenner and a significant player in *Keeping Up with the Kardashians*, he won a gold medal in the Olympics decathlon event in 1976. His book *Finding the Champion Within* fascinated me. I had never heard of anyone so committed! Every single day for four years he IMAGINED himself atop the gold medal platform, leaning over as they placed the heavy, shiny gold medal around his neck. He could hear the crowd cheering wildly all around him (SOUND). He felt ecstatic when he thought about this (EMOTION). His IMAGE was sensually rich and thus felt extremely real.

When he actually won the gold medal, he said it was so familiar — as if he had already been there. (And, as we will learn later in Part 3: "From Science to the Supernatural", he already had been there) Bruce Jenner used the energy principles of frequency, duration, and intensity to program his brain for the exact result he wanted — *to win a gold medal*.

TIP
A world without boundaries exists in your imagination

What victory are you ready to claim in your life? Where do you want to be a champion? What battles do you want to win? Whatever your desired victory is, you can create your own personal IMAGES to bring it forward from the infinite field of possibility, from the realm of unlimited potential into physical reality.

Mental Imagery Trains Your Brain for Top Performance

In *Psychology Today*, researcher Angie LeVan writes "Mental imagery impacts many cognitive processes in the brain: motor control, attention, perception, planning, and memory." When athletes use these techniques, the brain receives ongoing training for the actual athletic performance during visualization.

In 2013 my favorite NFL team from the pacific Northwest, where I lived, was the Seattle Seahawks. Interestingly, they added a mindfulness trainer to their professional staff because they recognized the immense value of this role. High-performance sports psychologist Michael Gervais tells them to "Quiet your minds," "Focus your attention inwardly," and "Visualize success." The unconventional move paid off: the Seahawks won the Super Bowl in 2014 just after they began these techniques.

Let's explore how their success can translate to your own. These mental practices will increase your confidence, motivation, and flow as well as prime your brain for success. What a wonderful list of positive qualities. Imagine:

- Confidence to give your next business presentation.
- Motivation to get up early and exercise.
- Flow to handle challenges with ease and grace.
- Belief you will earn excellent money for your talents.

You create a pattern in your brain that corresponds with what you want to achieve when you use IMAGES and visualize future results.

TIP: Brain Facts:
- You do not see with just your eyes, but with your brain.
- Your brain does not easily differentiate between what it sees visually outside and what it sees internally in the imagination.
- Your created IMAGES have the power to program your brain.

Inspired Visions and Mental Rehearsal Do Impact Peak Performance

Years ago, I read about an interesting man named Charles Garfield who related a fascinating story about his first job as an engineer at NASA. Fresh out of college, he found the environment stagnant when he arrived. Everyone plodded along doing their job — until President John F. Kennedy declared NASA would send a man to the moon and return him safely to earth by the end of the decade.

Whoa. Talk about a *vision* that inspired *massive action*. He said overnight everyone catapulted into high gear and never stopped until the mission was accomplished years later in 1969. They celebrated wildly this national success, a seemingly impossible dream come true. Garfield went on to say something strange happened next. Suddenly, the peak performance effort was over, the routine returned to business as usual, with little inspiration. This culture change affected Garfield to the point that he ended up quitting NASA and going back to college to study psychology, and later authored *Peak Performance*.

He was captivated that a powerful vision, when clearly articulated, could inspire such massive action and top-level performance. Without it, people tend to run on autopilot. Doesn't this help you to see the importance of creating a powerful vision for your life — *right now*?

Research on Soviet athletes demonstrated the power of mental training. The government-funded athletic programs all integrated sophisticated mental training, combined with rigorous physical training. One study evaluating these intensive programs suggests their potential. Four matched groups of world-class Soviet athletes diligently trained for many hours each week. The training regimens were as follows:

- Group I used 100 percent physical training.
- Group II used 75 percent physical training, 25 percent mental training.
- Group III used 50 percent physical training, 50 percent mental training.
- Group IV used 25 percent physical training, 75 percent mental training.

When the four groups were compared shortly before the 1980 Winter Games in Lake Placid, Group IV had shown significantly greater improvement than Group III, with Groups II and I following, in that order.

Are You Working Much Harder Than Necessary?

Think about the study's conclusion: mentally rehearsing excellent execution, along with lesser levels of physical action, is much more effective than 100 percent pure physical action. Is lack of mental rehearsal forcing you to exert more energy and time to projects without the results you seek? When you practice the **RISE to Success** ritual daily and add work to it, you will increase your performance exponentially. Making room in your schedule to spend 15 minutes per day with REPETITION – IMAGES – SOUND – EMOTION is a worthy time investment.

TIP

Your brain is waiting for the clear IMAGE of the future you desire

Let's explore how J.K. Rowling was inspired through IMAGES that popped into her life and helped her move forward with direction and action.

J.K. Rowling's Flash of Inspiration to Write Harry Potter Series

Rowling always loved to write and read. While riding homeward on a train, she suddenly saw an IMAGE in her mind of a boy who doesn't know he is a wizard, but goes to wizard school. The story unfolded quickly — bam, bam, bam. Interestingly, Rowling didn't have a pen to make notes in the moment, so she had to write down this incredible vision later. The *Harry Potter* series have sold over 400 million copies worldwide, with translation into 68 languages in over 200 territories.

Think about it: a phenomenon in young adult literature arose from a single inspired IMAGE.

You can **RISE** beyond your circumstances to create wealth and financial independence just as these people mentioned above did. They all started out as common folk who visualized a better life for themselves, using their special God-given talents and inspired ideas. They turned their dreams into reality and succeeded wildly.

So can you! They are not smarter than you — they just allowed themselves to **RISE to Success** through IMAGES of a better future. We have enough people who tell it like it is. Let's become people who tell it like *it could be*.

"At times our own light goes out and is rekindled by a spark from another person. Each of us has cause to think with deep gratitude of those who have lighted the flame within us."
— Albert Schweitzer, Humanitarian

We Get By With a Little IMAGING Help From Our Friends

In his book, *Positive Imaging*, Norman Vincent Peale relayed a touching story about someone who had a positive IMAGE of him when he was 19 years old. Frightened by a last-minute request to give a speech to 50,000 people on Memorial Day in the 1920's, he had arrived with the intention to give only the opening prayer. He firmly told the organizers he was not prepared for a speech and could not do it.

General Theodore Roosevelt, Jr., the guest of honor, overheard Peale's panic. He said, "Son, you are a minister, aren't you? You have a chance to minister to all these grieving people and tell them how much we love them for all the sacrifices they made, and how proud this country is of the husbands and sons they lost. So, get up there and talk. I will sit right behind you and visualize you loving these people and helping them and holding them spellbound for the next 20 minutes. I have a picture of this in my mind, and it's so strong, I know it is going to happen."

How heartwarming when Norman Vincent Peale, later known for his legendary book *The Power of Positive Thinking*, said, "Perhaps the idea of the power of positive thinking was conveyed to me right then

continued

and there." He said General Roosevelt's IMAGE of him succeeding must have been stronger than his own, because the talk went well.

Afterwards, General Roosevelt said, "Now, you see, if you think you can, or somebody who believes in you thinks you can, why, then you can!"

Think of me as that person who helps you hold a positive image of yourself so you can experience more victory in your life. I believe as you learn to consistently imagine yourself positively making a difference, making more money and living a good life, you will become unstoppable.

Three More Stories about the Power of Imaging and Visualizing

- While a street kid, Roger Ferger peeked in the window of the *Cincinnati Enquirer* and observed a man highly focused on his work. He decided, "I want to be him." He kept replaying that scene on his Image-screen until he became the editor of the *Cincinnati Enquirer* decades later.
- During World War II, a soldier recovered from near-fatal wounds by creating mental pictures of himself as a healthy, whole individual.
- Accused of being a spy by the Soviet Union, Natan Sharansky served a nine-year prison term. While in solitary confinement, Sharansky played against himself in mental chess. He said, "I might as well use the opportunity to become *the world champion*." Remarkably, after his release, he beat the current world champion chess player Garry Kasparov. Impressive — and all because of mental rehearsal.

What You Learned in Chapter 3:
IMAGES: Bring Vision Into Reality on Your "Image-screen"

Here is a quick review so far of how you will **RISE to Success**:

1. Use REPETITION to think over and over about what you want.
2. Craft IMAGES to bring your vision to life in a sensually rich mental movie.

Behind every success is the concept of IMAGES. That means projecting an image of yourself succeeding and visualizing it so vividly that when success comes, it seems to be an echo of a reality that already existed in your mind. Vital Point: *the brain does not know the difference between what is real and what is imagined*. Mental practice can get you closer to where you want to be in life. In short, it will help you to design the life you desire.

- The same brain regions are stimulated whether we visualize an action internally, or perform it externally (in reality).
- Your Image-screen is like a TV, phone, or laptop screen, but it exists in your mind.
- When you do creative IMAGING, use all your senses to bring it to life.
- Mentally rehearse specific aspects of the new person and the new life you want every day. With spaced REPETITION, you will program your brain for success.
- Increase the power, intensity, and duration of the vision of what you want, playing the mental movie for at least two minutes.
- You become what you imagine yourself to be — so make it *sensational*.

4 SOUND: You Will Have What You Say! The Power of Words

Words can be very powerful, filled with the potential to inspire results. We all have experienced the warmth that comes from well-chosen and uplifting words spoken by someone we care about. As well, we remember the sting of just a few hurtful words sent our way and the lingering impact of that resonance.

In this chapter on our **RISE to Success** journey, we enter the world of words that emit SOUND as they are spoken by us. When you construct daily spoken rituals as well as increase your awareness of what you say throughout the course of the day, you will reclaim your original voice. Your intentional voice will bring purposeful prosperity.

Use words wisely to help focus your thoughts. Develop speech patterns that will change your brain chemistry and bring forth events that you want. Language patterns are effective to help strengthen your thoughts:

- "I'm lucky."
- "Everything always works out fine."
- "All is well."
- "I expect miracles, and I get miracles."
- "I'm grateful for everything."

The late, great Muhammad Ali, heavyweight boxer and cultural icon of the 20th century was the master of positive declarations. With great bravado and flair, he modeled how to claim out loud what we want in our lives. He activated the SOUND section of the **RISE to Success** system. With his mantra *"I am the greatest!"* he lifted himself into another realm of reality and then lived up to his claims to become the boxing champion of the world.

In an interview he said, "I am not conceited, I am just convinced!" Yes, he was. What a powerful message lives in those words — let's be *convinced* of who we are and what we want in life. Let's have a high opinion of ourselves in a good way. Let's be noticed and remembered for the unique signature we bring to the world.

> "I am the greatest at what I do, there is nothing ordinary about me. I am a champion." — Muhammad Ali

The more you do your SOUND declarations on a daily basis, the more your confidence will grow, too. Just like Ali, you will become bolder about what you say. This is because REPETITION will change thoughts from a weak vibration to a stronger one. Once you form a dominant thought, you will *believe* it as *truth*. Once you believe what you say with conviction, and speak it frequently with intensity and power, it will activate the laws of nature. Things will begin to happen in your favor.

Use SOUND to Call Those Things You Want into Existence

Sound waves emanate from your mouth when you speak. These sound waves are never ending, like ripples on a pond. They go out into the atmosphere and dissipate, but never disappear unless cancelled by other sound waves. Now doesn't that give new meaning to the idea that what you say is quite important?

Have you ever heard the concept "call those things which be not, as though they are"? What this means is that we have the freedom and ability to use the SOUND of the words we speak

TIP
Your "mountain" will obey you — Your mountain needs to hear your voice!

and call things we want into existence. You will have what you say! Words have the power of life and death in them, blessing and cursing, of creation and destruction. What are you choosing to say, to speak, to voice — and what is the impact on your relationships, your success, your results, and your life?

What is the "mountain" in your life right now? Is it related to finances, relationships, health, career, spirituality, emotions, or mental state? You are the one who needs to declare to your mountain what you want to happen. You have more control than you might imagine you do with the words that you speak. In effect, your voice is a powerful creative force.

Your Voice is the Substance That Will Turn Your Vision into Reality

What do you have faith for in your life? What do you believe is possible for your future? When everything seems bleak, overwhelming, too hard, too much, what do you do? You can use your voice to call forth what you want. The SOUND must come out of *your* mouth, with *your* unique voice, and in words crafted by *you* to declare and emphasize what you want to create in life.

I heard about a woman named Nancy who had been out of the workplace for over twenty years. She really wanted a job but had spoken out loud all her life that she lacked marketable talent. The echo of those words reverberated throughout her life. Recently, with the help of mentors, she shifted her paradigm by adopting a new belief. Nancy decided she has incredible value and worth in the marketplace due to her impeccable relationship skills and abilities. Now her new, empowering language cancels out the previous negative identity and limited view of herself. She spoke out loud about her positive qualities, and landed a job based on what she was saying and believing about herself. She is now successful and happy in her job.

The lesson here is to carefully watch your words. Watch what you say about yourself. And watch what you say *to yourself*. Be conscious of what you speak about your circumstances, your future, your success, and the state of the world in general.

If you want to complain, please think twice. After 2016 the political climate has became quite charged, with negatively spoken words from various camps. Consider this: will your critical words help anyone or will they just add to the pessimism already out there? When I read *Secrets of the Millionaire Mind* by successful businessman T. Harv Eker, I chuckled when he said that when you complain, you become a "crap magnet." It is a funny saying, but it rings true. Eker's comment is an emotional anchor for me. When I think about complaining, I remind myself of this and stop. Who wants to attract more "crap"?

Speak Positively about What You Want

Line up your words with what you want to "be-do-have" in your life. Every day, every waking moment, speak positively about what you want to create. It's so easy to become numb to our words much of the time. If we say, "I can't," "I won't," or "I'll never," we are creating a self-fulfilling prophecy.

Avoid claims of what you don't want:

- "I am terrible at relationships."
- "I can't afford that."
- "I am so discouraged."
- "I am really bad at holding onto money."
- "I will never get ahead."
- "I am so stressed out."

Watch the Negative Words Spoken in Our Everyday Lives

As I took a break from writing this book, I encountered a friend's boyfriend who gave me a valuable real-world example of this very principle. He explained why he could not help her lift something heavy because of pain affecting his sciatica. He said, "I am always hurting myself. It happens all the time." He was so matter of fact while making this negative declaration that I could not help but notice.

Typically, I would not make a corrective comment to someone I barely knew. However, being immersed in this chapter, I could not help myself. I heard myself saying to him, "Cancel, Cancel." My positively minded colleagues and I have been trained to utter this phrase when we hear ourselves or someone else say something negative. I added, "What you just said is not want you want, and your words are powerful and will reinforce this."

As I noticed the look on his face, I caught myself, and apologized. I explained my deep dive into researching and writing about this very thing: the power of what we say out loud can impact our lives.

I was quite surprised when he went on to validate his ingrained beliefs by saying, "Well, I am a guy, and guys always hurt themselves when they are working. That's just the way it is." Wow. Okay. I just smiled and realized that was the end of the conversation. And I mentally thanked him for a fitting example to share with my audience.

When you go through tough times and constantly speak about them, it causes you to think about them in a running thought stream. You will continue to feel bad and potentially produce even more challenging times. Break the pattern by changing what you think and how you speak. I have even heard a suggestion to set a limit of 3x to talk about anything "bad" that happened and then to move on. Don't get stuck in an endless recounting of "poor me".

Have you ever unknowingly spoken what you don't want or what you fear, and then some time later something very bad happens to you or someone you love? Let's explore the possibility that SOUND from words impacts our lives. In Part 3: "Beyond Science to the Supernatural", we will discover the science that lies at the root of this situation. For instance, worry can become a pattern that repeats itself so often it spirals out of control and to the point you will manifest physical symptoms. Worry statements can truly set negative goals. Worry happens when you focus on what you *don't want* to happen.

How My Near-Death Experience in High School Came From A Negative Focus

I learned a valuable lesson about the consequences that result from what we speak about and focus on — positive or negative. As a high school senior, I was hospitalized at The National Institute of Health (NIH) in Washington, D.C. Local tests in my home state of Ohio revealed I had kidney-related high blood pressure because of a birth defect. The deformed valve caused a back flow of toxins from a third ureter to a third kidney. The kidney became scarred and damaged, triggering high blood pressure as it attempted to pump more blood to the affected area. I was immediately sent to NIH to become part of a government research study on this condition.

My father, who loved me very much, was a first class "worrier." I made it through the intricate surgery to remove my extra kidney and ureter and rested well in intensive care alongside heart-transplant patients. My father came to visit and shared with me that, because I had so many allergies, he was "worried sick" that I would have an allergic reaction to the blood transfusion they were administering. I listened, and in my medicated state, my subconscious mind easily registered his intense fear. My dad truly did not want this to happen to me, yet this was exactly where his intense focus was and what he spoke out loud.

Shortly after he left the room, I noticed my skin felt rather strange and itchy. I rang the little bell the nurses had given me, and a crotchety nurse came over and sternly informed me, "You are the second least important person in this intensive care unit, and we will get

continued

to you when we have time!" Then she stormed off. I reached to my back and felt some very large lumps (hives). Suddenly, my eyes swelled shut, and I screamed, "Help!"

A team of nurses yanked me out of bed onto a chair and gave me multiple shots of norepinephrine because I was officially in anaphylactic shock. The hives covered my entire body. All of this happened because of a life-threatening allergic reaction to the blood transfusion. To this day, I believe my father focused so strongly on what *he didn't want to happen,* that he clearly and intently imagined it into reality. He transmitted this fear into the atmosphere around him, including me.

My doctor told me I was much closer to dying at that moment than at any time of the lengthy surgery. Of course, I was relieved to still be among the living, and so was everyone around me, especially my family. Later I would learn that this life-threatening event is classified as a "near death experience," which forever changed me.

The moral of the story: It makes sense to watch our thoughts and words very carefully and stay laser focused on what we *want* to happen, and not on what we *don't want* to happen. Strive to be more aware and speak words that are positive 90 percent of the time.

This is what it sounds like to claim what you *do want*:

- "Something *good* is going to happen to me today!"
- "I am full of energy and vitality."
- "I have and enjoy fantastic relationships."
- "My mind is sharp and clear, and I remember things easily."
- "I am excited to see my bank accounts increase dramatically."
- "I am a valuable member of a team, family, and community."
- "I am blessed in the city and in the country."

In the **RISE to Success Journal** in Part 4: "How to **RISE to Success** in 15 Minutes Per Day", we will delve into more specific examples and insights on how to design your personalized declarations. When you repeat SOUND declarations daily, you will speak positivity into your life and thereby program your brain for success.

The Miracle of How SOUND Is Sent and Received Biologically

When you talk to a friend, here is a breakdown of what really happens:

From your brain to your friend's ear:

- Your brain has a thought.
- That thought is translated into a pattern of pressure waves.
- Your lungs send air out of your body, and you vibrate your vocal chords.
- You move your mouth and tongue into shape to form the sound.
- High- and low-pressure patterns code the air and continue to spread out.

From your friend's ear to your friend's brain:

- A little bit of that air ends up in your friend's ears, and the eardrums vibrate.
- The eardrums transmit information into an electrical impulse.
- The electrical impulse reaches the auditory nerve and then the brain.
- The brain decodes the information.
- Your friend receives the thought.

All of this transpires in one-eighth of a second with no effort from either of you. *Think about the ramifications of this process*. The thoughts we *think* are intertwined with our *spoken words*. They are synergistic. They work together and impact our lives greatly. Therefore, we are wise to choose *positive* thoughts and *positive* words. These choices are made in our conscious mind and influence our body, mind, and spirit. (Explanation rephrased from Tim Urban's *Wait but Why* blog post on March 9, 2016 titled "Everything You Should Know About Sound")

Using Spoken Declarations to Demolish Debt

In the introduction, I related how I got out of debt quickly. I used **RISE to Success** after the 2008–2010 recession hit my coaching and training business hard. Let me share with you one example of how I used SOUND to make that happen.

As you can imagine, there was a fair amount of stress and anxiety when my income disappeared, and I was already in over my head financially. Of course, this occurred before I learned the strategies I share with you to manage emotional states. Nonetheless, I noticed that as I began to speak my declarations more often and more intensely, my fear and anxiety lowered dramatically. What a relief it was to experience this right away.

I stuck to a daily routine. Just down the hill from my house, I walked or rode my bike to the large concrete walking bridge over the Spokane River. As the river roared beneath me and birds soared overhead, I spoke out my declarations with passion and energy. "I am the head and not the tail, above and not beneath. I will lend to many nations, but I will not have to borrow!" This is a powerful ancient text from the bible I resonate with.

Some days I repeated this statement over 20 times, imagining and feeling what it would be like to be completely out of debt, with enough money to give to others. With vigor, I shouted so loud every cell of my body would listen. Within a relatively short time I was out of debt. And one day after giving to the *International Healing Rooms*, I realized I was lending money to the nations. Now that was a good feeling.

Are you willing to put your heart and soul into this? When you do, you will get results.

We Are 90 Percent Water, So Be Careful What You Say

In the book *Hidden Messages of Water*, Dr. Masaru Emoto introduces his revolutionary work. Emoto is an internationally known Japanese scientist and alternative health doctor. The dazzling experiments he conducted and their results could very well cause a paradigm shift in your view of the impact of words on your life.

Dr. Emoto discovered that crystals formed in frozen water reveal changes when thoughts and words from human brains are directed toward them. He photographed water at a molecular level and then several people proceeded to think thoughts to the water, tape words on the water, play music to the water, and pray blessings over the water. He viewed the changes in the physical structure of water under a microscope.

Here are several visible effects he claims these practices had on the structure of the water:

1. Uplifting words/pure water created complex and gorgeous snowflake patterns.
2. Harsh words/polluted water created disruptive, asymmetrical patterns.
3. Positive words made brilliant images while negative words made dark, dull ones.
4. The impact of words spoken in love/appreciation can be seen with our own eyes.

LOVE

HATE

If you remember from high school science class, our bodies are 90 percent water. What do Emoto's experiments mean for you and me in our everyday lives? Could every thought, feeling, and word impact our bodies more deeply than we can imagine?

Dr. Emoto says, "The implications of this research create a new awareness of how we can positively impact the earth and our personal health." Even though Emoto's studies have not withstood double blind studies to prove their efficacy, his experiments are nevertheless thought provoking.

Sound Can Also Be Used for Healing in Some Very Unique Ways

When I was using *The Healing Code* discovered by psychologist and naturopath Dr. Alex Loyd, part of the process called for "truth focus statements" to be spoken out loud. The purpose was to cancel out lies in my subconscious mind with positive word vibrations while doing quantum mechanical hand movements around my face. For me this was a very simple process that worked exceedingly well.

Some alternative medicine doctors use sound to modulate brain wave patterns and synchronize the right and left hemispheres of the brain. This can help with stress reduction, heart disease, depression, and other conditions. The basis of these processes is the fact that every tissue in the body and every physical object will resonate to very specific SOUND frequencies that the nervous systems will "hear". The experience of sound is at the very core of human consciousness and is a powerful tool for healing,

Recently I had an experience of a unique type of sound healing therapy. My close friend and pianist, Carla Reed, uses tuning forks to facilitate healing. I have to say I have never felt so tranquil as she "pinged" the tuning forks and then held them within inches of my ear as I was lying on a massage table. Immediately my whole body relaxed at a very deep level due to the subtle sound vibration.

To review our **RISE to Success** simple daily system so far:

1. Use REPETITION to think about what you want over and over.
2. Craft IMAGES to bring your vision to life in a sensually rich mental movie.
3. Speak and say words to generate SOUND vibrations that create what you want.

What You Learned in Chapter 4:
SOUND: You Will Have What You Say! The Power of Words

SOUND from the words that we speak out loud is very powerful. We can make positive declarations daily over our lives and see physical manifestations occur. When you repeat SOUND declarations daily, you will speak positivity into your life and thereby program your brain for success. Your confidence will grow, and then you will become bolder about what you say. This is because REPETITION will change your thoughts from weak to strong. Eventually you will *believe* it as true.

- Use your words to speak what you *want* — not what you *don't want.*
- Positive thoughts and words program your subconscious mind.
- Use SOUND to call those things you want into existence.
- The more positive declarations you make, the more you will begin to believe them and expect them to become true.
- Your voice is the substance that will turn your vision into reality.
- Positive words made brilliant images while negative words made dark, dull ones.
- You can train yourself to speak positively about circumstances in your life, events, people, and current affairs. Go for 90 percent positive!

5 EMOTION: Feel Good to Pull Positive Results To You Quickly

Positive and Negative "Vibes" Attract and Repel People

Almost everyone is familiar with the concept of positive and negative "vibes." Think about the most positive people in your life — the kind of people who uplift you, who put you in a good mood just being around them. You enjoy being in their presence, don't you? Then there are the people who always seem to have a cloud over their head, kind of like the old cartoon characters who shuffle around and are depressed and negative most of the time. It is almost as if they carry a rain cloud with them, and being around them feels heavy.

Can you think of any places — homes, stores, coffee shops and the "good vibe" you feel when you enter? Some of these places give you a sense of excitement, love, connectedness, and belonging, all positive.

What EMOTION do you feel around people who are either positive or negative? What EMOTION do you feel inside yourself when you are positive or negative or any variation in between? I confess sometimes it's easier for me to recognize emotional states in *others* than it is myself. I don't always realize what kind of "vibe" I am emanating. I can get so caught up in what is happening that I don't realize

TIP
The more often you tune in to your "vibe," the easier it will become to identify what you are feeling and take steps to feel better

I have become frustrated or sad or overwhelmed. In turn, I speak and act in a less than optimal way. Sound familiar?

As I have become much more convinced that my EMOTION is directly related to my results, I have significantly improved. Now I am more aware how I feel *and* take responsibility and control over it.

Can you think of a time when you weren't aware that the stress from work, school, family challenges, finances, and everything else you might encounter in life brought you down? Depending on your level of self-awareness and emotional intelligence, you may or may not be able to tune into your emotional state at any given moment. Let's be frank — this does come easier to some people than others.

Every single moment becomes an opportunity to change your life, because in any split second you can change the way you feel. Feelings are often simply programs — subconscious automatic programs of how we react to the external world. Many of them were designed to help us survive. Many of them were ingrained in us at an early age.

When you are joyful, when you say, "Yes" to life and project positivity all around you, you become a shining light in a sometimes dark world, and people want to be near you.

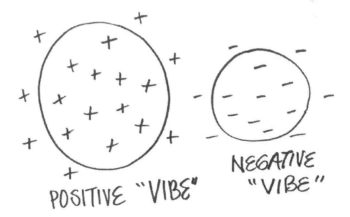

POSITIVE "VIBE"   NEGATIVE "VIBE"

Super Top-Secret Insight about the Power of Your Emotions

Let's just get to the significant point about this chapter on EMOTION and how feeling good helps us to **RISE to Success**. I am going to share with you something very few people in this world know because they have never been made aware of this fact. This super top-secret insight will change your life in this very second, if you open your mind and let it in. (see TIP)

> **TIP**
>
> Your number one goal every moment of every day is to *feel good now* and keep feeling better.

Do this one thing, and you will become a magnet for positive results:

- Wake each day excited. Open your eyes, jump out of bed, and say, "Something good is going to happen to me today!"
- Feeling good means being outrageously happy. The more you practice being happy, the more it becomes a habit, and you eventually reach unconscious competence and feel bliss, enthusiasm, elation, and joy.
- Realize that complaining, blaming, criticizing, and talking badly about other people and events will affect *you* the most — because it makes *you* feel bad.
- Get a burning desire and excitement for your goals and dreams; this happens when you feel good about them and believe deep down they can happen.

Positive thinking is important, positive words are important, and positive action is important. But nothing compares to your ability to generate positive "vibes" and feel good. How you feel inside and what you project on the outside sets up an energy vibration and attracts to you circumstances, events, and people who are a match to that exact level. In Part 3: "Beyond Science to the Supernatural", we will look at the how this actually works. I think you will be as stunned as I was, to learn these intriguing facts.

You are capable (as I have been) to reinvent yourself and become the person you want to become. What do you have to change to live in joy? The moment we ask such a question, the brain activates and interrupts the automatic program. *Now we can make a new choice.* We really do create our own destiny; good or bad.

We Need to Take 100 Percent Responsibility for Our Lives

Our outside circumstances have little to do with the things we consider bad and negative in our life. Incredibly, our past negative "vibes" have brought most of this on. When we feel bad, those negative "vibes" come right back around to us in interesting ways. We are able to choose our responses to everything that happens, lift our emotions up, and create a happier and more joyful life.

How do You Keep Feeling Good Even With Life's Challenges?

While I was writing this book, friends referred by to a mechanic. He did some tune-up work on my van that I had driven all over the country until I landed in California. The day ended up as a comedy of errors: with me forgetting something at home, having to back-track, me leaving my keys to my office on the keychain with him, more backtracking, him leaving his cell phone in my van, more backtracking, and then finally the parts he replaced did not fix the problem. As we stood there with the engine hood up, he said, "Don't be upset, Patrice. I will make this right."

I was doing a 10-day cleanse at the time, and I did feel a bit off with the detox happening in my bloodstream. I was tired and hot in the intense California sun. I purposefully shifted my state, looked him in the eye, smiled widely, and said, "This is exactly what I am writing about in the book I mentioned to you. Whatever happens we have to believe it will work out and not get upset emotionally. Because the emotion we send out will impact our lives and come back to us."

"Really" he said. "Wow. Maybe you should tell that to Gary (our mutual friend). He is always so negative and upset about every-thing." We both laughed because it was true. The mechanic, I had observed, is an easy-going, positive guy who has five kids and a lot on his plate. But he seemed to be such a happy-go-lucky person.

continued

I said, "This is nothing in the big scheme of life!"

Then we talked about some real tragedies that had just happened in our town and the horrible time these people were having. We both agreed that would be tough to deal with, but this auto issue was really nothing, *and it would all work out.*

We shared more stories and sentiments, and this experience became quite a bonding moment as we kept our positive "vibe" very high. I shared that I wanted to sell the seven-passenger van and buy a smaller SUV. He said he was ready to upgrade his vehicle (with his family of seven), and he would be open to buying it. Well, that just made me smile and feel even happier. I felt quite content and satisfied as I drove away.

Wonderful how this works, so stay positive and attract what you want.

Let's pause a moment to recap the steps in our **RISE to Success** process:

- Use REPETITION to think about what you want over and over.
- Craft IMAGES to bring your vision to life in a sensually rich mental movie.
- Speak and say words to generate SOUND vibrations that create what you want.
- Pay attention to your EMOTIONS and feel good most of the time.

Since our goal is now to consistently seek good vibrations emanating from within us to the outside world, it is helpful to review a list of emotions and become aware of where they fall from high "vibes" to low "vibes."

TIP
When you feel *bad*, you are vibrating at a low level
When you feel *good*, you are vibrating at a high level

Range of Emotions (from highest to lowest):

- Love
- Exuberance/bliss
- Joy
- Appreciation
- Exhilaration
- Empowerment
- Freedom
- Passion
- Enthusiasm
- Happiness
- Eagerness
- Positive expectation
- Belief
- Optimism
- Security
- Hopefulness
- Confidence
- Contentment
- Boredom
- Pessimism
- Frustration
- Irritation
- Impatience
- Overwhelm
- Disappointment
- Doubt
- Worry
- Blame
- Discouragement
- Anger
- Revenge
- Hatred/Rage
- Jealousy
- Insecurity/guilt/unworthiness
- Anxiety
- Fear
- Grief
- Depression
- Despair
- Powerlessness

Learn to monitor how you feel. The ability to feel "really good" consistently is an essential indicator that you are on the right track.

You can control your EMOTIONS. Pay attention and let your emotions be the valuable indicators that they are. Be thankful you have such a clear guidance system giving you immediate feedback about your "vibe". Thank you *anger*, thank you *frustration*, thank you *anxiety*; you help me to realize I need to shift to *feeling good*.

The goal is not to go from "depressed" to "elated" but to move a couple steps up the scale from where you are currently. If you are generally a "positive energy person," it doesn't mean you won't ever feel sad or unhappy. The difference is to not let yourself be defined by your negative mood; then you will be able to make the shift upward.

We are always feeling something. We are always emoting something. The higher up, the better. But what about when real upsets happen and it affect us emotionally — spiraling us down . . . down . . . down? A tropical storm approaches, a customer is disgruntled, a friend is diagnosed with cancer, or you get a letter from a lawyer about a business deal.

The key is to move just a couple steps up the ladder, not to go from the bottom to the top in one moment — from despair to exhilaration. If you feel despair, well then, angry is better. There is more juice. There is more energy. It is not ideal, but remember, your goal is to feel better incrementally until you rise from anger to hopefulness, from positive expectation to empowerment. And finally you arrive to the state of joy, love and appreciation, the highest vibration emotions.

How do you do this? Good question. Since this may be a new awareness, here is a list:

Strategies to Improve Your Emotional State and Feel Better

1. Gratitude
2. The Mind Switch
3. Emotional Anchors
4. Immediate Actions

1. Gratitude is the Easiest Way to Feel Better Now

The fastest way to immediately feel good is to be grateful for the people, things, and juicy wonders of your life. Being grateful puts out a "vibe" of love, appreciation and thankfulness. People, events and circumstances that match these feeling vibrations will start to come into your life. Mountains will start to move as a result and you will receive more of what you are sending out. Then you will feel even more thankful.

This technique is so *simple* and works instantly because you cannot possibly feel "bad" when you are thinking about what you are grateful for and writing it down. The reason I created the **RISE to Success Journal** is for you to have a structure and place to do this every day. (More details are found in Chapter 19: "How to RISE with EMOTION")

In the 1990s, Harvard lecturer Shawn Achor conducted the largest-ever study on happiness and human potential. In his book *The Happiness Advantage,* he outlines seven principles for improving performance and gaining a competitive edge at work. One of Achor's most remarkable discoveries was also one of the most practical: *People who practice gratitude every day are happier and more optimistic.*

TIP
Gratitude = Happiness

There are now thousands of scientific studies that confirm the benefit of gratitude. Many famous people and successful entrepreneurs practice gratitude as part of their morning ritual:

- Oprah Winfrey, TV personality, producer and media mogul
- Richard Branson, Founder of *Virgin Records*, billionaire
- Tim Ferris, Author, jetsetter, successful entrepreneur
- John Paul DeJoria, Founder and creator of *Paul Mitchell* hair salons
- Tony Robbins, Peak performance coach, successful entrepreneur
- Jack Canfield, Author *Chicken Soup for the Soul*, transformation leader
- Lisa Nichols, Motivational speaker, author and successful entrepreneur

"For the most part, I can't tell you how important it is to take those first five minutes of the day and be thankful for life."
— John Paul DeJoria

To achieve more, to be happy, and to make a difference, practice gratitude. Have you ever met an unhappy person who is grateful for their life or a happy person who isn't grateful? Happiness is not a place you can travel to, own, earn, or consume. Living every moment with love, grace and gratitude puts you on the spiritual path to happiness.

The simplest way to create a magical life is to transmit feelings of gratitude. Feel grateful for the people, things, and other aspects of your life. Everyone, everywhere, whatever your circumstances, has many, many things to be grateful for!

It doesn't matter if you own a Rolls Royce, a private jet, or an island in the Caribbean; if you are depressed, have cancer, and don't talk to your kids anymore, who cares about all the stuff? What really matters is *how you feel*. Do you wake up every day excited to be on this planet and enjoying the roller coaster ride of life? Are you exhilarated by the challenge and adventure of every moment? This is where the treasure chest with all the gold nuggets is found.

Where Are the Happiest People?

Even in the remote tribes of Ethiopia, many people are very happy because they have learned to enjoy the simple pleasures of life: water to drink, rice to eat, and a new baby being born. A smile from a friend and a good night's sleep nestled next to loved ones brings abundant joy.

2. The Mind Switch – Flip the Switch from Negative to Positive

One technique I have learned is called the "Mind Switch". The way this works is that when something appears to be "bad" you can make a decision to take that event from negative to positive. You can flip an imaginary switch in your mind from *lights off* to *lights on*, from *dark* to *light*. Your mind is capable of making this switch, and you can develop this habit and feel better immediately. Here are a few things you need to do:

- Relax
- Take a deep breath
- Take a bigger picture view of the situation
- Make a decision to flip the switch to positive
- Lift your emotional state to a higher level

This makes life a lot more fun because you are able to live without anxiety and angst. When life throws you a curveball you are able to respond in a positive way — no matter what.

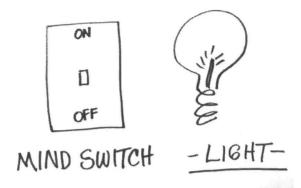

MIND SWITCH   - LIGHT -

Finding the Silver Lining in Any Dark Cloud

Recently I was at a garden party, and I met a woman who was the poster child for this strategy. I had heard about her before I met her. She lives next door to my friend who held the party, and my friend shared with me that she moved to Northern California from Florida after her husband had committed suicide by shooting himself. Her children, ages 9 and 11, were with her as they all tried to revive him. Now that is a lot of trauma to experience. When I met this lovely woman, instead of depression and sadness, I experienced someone who was optimistic, hopeful, and dreaming about her future. This was only three months after her heartbreaking experience.

She told me she made a decision to appreciate all the love he had shown her, how well he treated her, and especially the children they had created together. She believed in her heart that their 26 years together were an incredible gift, and the best way to honor his memory was to move on and create a new life with her children and their extended family. Wow — impressive. She spent most of our time together expressing passion for her healing work as a nurse practitioner. What a joy to be around her because she was so positive. She had flipped her "Mind Switch" from the dark to the light.

You see this with toddlers all the time. They can be wailing and flopping around on the floor as if the world is coming to an end. Next thing you know someone or something catches their attention and immediately they shift. A smile beams across their face before the tears even have a chance to dry, because they have an instant "Mind Switch".

Recently I heard an interesting account of welterweight world champion Manny Pacquiao. Manny is also a good example of just how capable our brains are of activating the ability to shift gears emotionally. This is a bit of a reverse story, however.

Manny was observed before a title fight laughing and joking around with the crowd. He had a big smile on his face and looked more like he was at a birthday party than a fight. But when the bell rang, he became a punching turbine ready to destroy anyone who stepped in front of him. He activated his "Mind Switch" in a different way, yet he demonstrated we all have this same ability to change our mental state — if we choose to use it. Make a note of this technique and when the opportunity comes around, flip your mind switch to positive.

3. Emotional Anchors – Take Your Emotions to the Mountaintop

I have climbed a lot of mountains in my life. The first one I climbed, as a teenager, was Table Mountain in Tennessee . . . in the fog! When we reached the top, we could barely see our hands in front of our faces, but I will never forget the feeling of accomplishment as I stood at the peak of that mountain. Once I moved West, I had the opportunity to climb many more, and it is unbelievable to stand at the top and gaze at the vista of land, distant mountains, and sky spread out before you. The emotion is one of true exhilaration.

Can you remember a moment when you felt absolutely on top of the world? Even if you have never climbed an actual mountain, we all have mountaintop experiences we can reconnect with in our life. Tap into that memory and experience the same EMOTION now. When I do this activity in workshops, I hear people talk about the birth of their children, graduation from college, their wedding day, a well-received presentation, a new job, or a moment as simple as standing back to enjoy a newly refurbished 1974 Dodge Charger.

In my life, I remember a trip back to Ohio to surprise my younger cheerleader sister at the start of her homecoming parade; climbing Lone Peak at *Big Sky* on skis for the first time and skiing down the south face with my closest friends; getting married at a pristine high mountain lake six miles up a backcountry trail with 24 people to help us celebrate; and also giving a speech at a major conference and receiving multiple standing ovations.

When we think of these experiences, we can revive the powerful positive emotions they generated initially. The moment you think about it, you are inspired with a surge of positive energy and brain chemicals that ignite your internal "feel good" and "I love life" buttons. Can you feel it?

The next step is to think about new experiences you envision happening, that are now filled with these same positive feelings. This will release more chemicals into your brain — *wiring you for success*. When you reach a happy place within yourself in the "now" moment and then dream about a positive future, this is an excellent formula for manifestation. Visualize what is possible:

- Advance to director of your department.
- Buy a new Mercedes.
- Release extra 15 pounds of body fat.
- Restore your relationship with your mother.
- Finish your book.
- Travel to Tuscany.
- Coach your kids' soccer team to a championship win.

4. Immediate Actions Shift Your "Vibe" to a Higher Level

Radiating positive "vibes" and living a happy lifestyle isn't difficult when you take action each day to find your balance and promote positive feelings over negative ones. Immediate action steps to improve your "vibe" can make a large

TIP
When you feel down or low, do something to shift your energy higher

difference in not just your life, but also in the lives of others around you. This is the most responsible and conscious thing to do because this way you don't bring others down to your level. Once you are aware you are feeling down, discouraged, angry, fearful, resentful, or hurt, you can take some immediate actions to feel better.

Remember: it is about moving up the emotional scale, one or two steps at a time, with the goal of *feeling better*, not necessarily blissful. In Part Four: "How to **RISE to Success** in 15 Minutes per Day", you will have more in-depth examples. For now, here are a few categories and examples in which you can take immediate action.

- Physical – Breathe, stretch, walk, get a massage, eat high "vibe" foods
- Mental – Journal, meditate, read a good book, write poetry, watch a movie
- Emotional – Clear limiting beliefs, use energy healing techniques, seek counsel
- Spiritual – Pray, meditate, attend a spiritual service, serve others in need
- Relational – Call a friend, pet your dog, get a hug, go to a high "vibe" party, share

It is smart if you take action to keep your EMOTION at a higher level. You can learn how to take control of your emotional state and interrupt any habitual negative processes before they do harm in your life. You can choose instead positive, uplifting actions that will lift you to a higher and happier level.

We have reached the conclusion of the four-parts of **RISE to Success**:

1. REPETITION: You Become What You Think About Most Often.
2. IMAGES: Bring Vision into Reality on Your Image-screen.
3. SOUND: You Will Have What You Say! The Power of Words.
4. EMOTION: Feel Good to Pull Positive Results to You Quickly.

What You Learned in Chapter 5:
EMOTIONS: Feel Good to Pull Positive Results to You Quickly

Your number one goal every moment of every day is to *feel good* now and *keep feeling better*! Your EMOTIONS directly influence your health, your finances, your relationships, your career, and, in general, the overall quality of your life. The more you become aware of your emotional state, the easier it will become to identify what you are feeling and take steps to feel better. When you are able to maintain a happy and healthy mindset most of the time, you will create positive results in all areas of your life.

- Your positive "vibes" attract to you the people, events, and opportunities you desire.
- Your negative "vibes" repel people, events, and opportunities away from you.
- Feelings are often subconscious programs of how we respond to the world. With repetition and awareness, we can develop new habits for better results.
- Gratitude will shift your emotional state to positive the fastest. Every day identify at least three things for which you are thankful.
- The "Mind Switch" is something you can flip from dark to light, from negative to positive by how you view your life circumstances and manage your emotions.
- Create emotional anchors by linking positive mountaintop memories from your past to future dreams and desires.
- Take immediate actions physically, mentally, emotionally, spiritually, and relationally to feel better.

PART 2

POSITIVE RESULTS
FROM THE INSIDE OUT

Easy Math Formula Predicts Your Likelihood to Change 6

To effectively use the **RISE to Success** system, it starts with the desire to create positive change in your life. Do you want more money, more opportunity, more passion and purpose? Do you want to move to a better city or house, or drive a different car? Do you want to feel amazing, have more energy, and leap tall buildings in a single bound?

Whatever you want to change in your life — use this super easy math formula and results will be delivered pronto. Who knew that the key to change in your life is based on a powerful and simple "Formula for Change"? This will be explained in detail in this chapter. In simple language, here is how it works: The Vision you have for your life is multiplied by what brings Dissatisfaction to you, and added to the First Steps you take to make the change. This combination must be greater than any Resistance you have that holds you back from the change. That's it!

Most People Just Want to Hang Out in Their Comfort Zone

Let's face it — generally speaking, people don't like change. Change forces us out of our comfort zone and many of us really like to be comfortable. The mother afraid to get back into the workforce, the man in a dead-end job he hates, the abused spouse who can't imagine leaving are all stuck in their comfort zone. Many people go to the grave filled with regrets and unhappy they didn't do some things differently. What is really crazy is many people want and expect to do better, but they don't change their thinking, behavior, habits, or their rituals to get different results. I believe they call that insanity, right? It's doing the "same old, same old", and expecting better results. We so easily fall back into old habits . . .

RISE Helps You Make Simple Changes in Your Daily Habits

This book is about making simple changes in your daily habits that will give you positive results. When you are only *interested* you will likely not change. When you are *committed* you will do whatever it takes to alter how you think and feel, and shift what you *do* every day to make the positive changes to live the life you want. You simply have to decide and then take *action*.

> "A real decision is measured by the fact that you've taken a new action. If there's no action, you haven't truly decided."
> — Tony Robbins, *Unlimited Power*

The brand *Chicken Soup for the Soul* eventually sold over 500 million copies. Initially, co-authors Jack Canfield and Mark Victor Hansen set a goal to sell 2 million books and both consistently took five actions each day to make it happen. Actions included radio interviews, sending the book out to editors to review, getting press releases written, etc. They each had a card in their pockets with their goal to sell 2 million books. They reviewed this card every day. As well, they created a mock-up of an image of their book in the #1 spot on *New York Times* bestseller list. Every day they looked at this image and visualized and felt what it would be like for *Chicken Soup for the Soul* to be at the top of the list. They achieved the goal, which took them two years. Both of them were totally committed to their vision and took massive action to make it happen.

Are You That Special Person Who Really Wants Positive Change?

Because you are reading this book right now, I am certain you are one of the special people who really wants to create positive change — *the few, the evolved and the brave.* I am honored to show you what has worked for me. I can save you a lot of time and headaches. Because I have risen above so many challenges in my life, because I have a system that is proven to work, and because I am a "Queen of Change", there is likely no one better to assist you than me. Once you understand and apply this change formula, and blend it with the **RISE to Success** daily system, you will literally be supercharged for success.

YOUR FORMULA FOR CHANGE IS MADE UP OF 4 ELEMENTS

$$(V \times D) + F > R$$

V - VISION

Precision. Clarity. Vision. New Identity. WHAT YOU WANT to Be-Do-Have in your life. (V) Represents vision. How well have you visualized positive change you want? Have you seen it on your Image-screen? How does it make you feel? What are the juicy details? Start by creating a powerful vision of what you want. The more juice, the more high vibration feelings, and the more clarity you imagine, the stronger and more powerful your vision will be. How can you make your vision even stronger, more empowering, and more desirable?

D - DISSATISFACTION

Frustration. Anxiety. Boredom. What really bugs you about your current situation? What kind of PAIN are you feeling in your body and your mind? Have you slipped into a comfort zone and don't really feel any dissatisfaction (D)? If so, then like a hammock, you have just laid back into it over and over. If you are complacent, you will not change; you are "OK" with the way things are. How can you increase your level of dissatisfaction? What would make the pain higher? Dissatisfaction is what gives us the *courage* to make a change in our life.

Vision (V) and Dissatisfaction (D) work together, in concert with each other. The greater and more compelling your vision at an emotional level, the greater your level of dissatisfaction will be. That is why they are bracketed and multiplied together. Combined, the V and

D represent the emotional "WHY" behind changing. That's critical because your "WHY" has to be big enough and strong enough to seek out the next component — the first steps (F).

F - FIRST STEPS

What do I do now? You may or may not have to figure out the first steps (F) to achieve your vision. This is the "HOW", and just like in the story of my journey out west you are about to read, I was so clear about my vision, that the people, opportunities and circumstance were drawn to me and presented themselves as I began to speak out my vision to others. First steps are the action steps you will take to move forward toward your vision. Typically, nothing will happen without action. And massive action creates momentum.

"The secret of getting ahead is getting started." — Mark Twain

---

R - RESISTANCE

Fear. Doubt. Unbelief. Uncertainty. Discomfort. The (R) represents your resistance to change — the block to your Vision becoming a reality. Just so you know, this is often the biggest barricade to your success. The real culprit can be outside of your conscious awareness. Limiting beliefs lurk beneath the surface and put up a major road-block to your dream. All of the barriers to change stand their ground in resistance, and keep you doing the same thing — the comfortable thing, the familiar thing, the safe, the practical thing. (Ugh! I truly hate this part and since I am super familiar with this, I can certainly help you out here, too.)

Joe Dispenza wrote a revolutionary book called *Breaking the Habit of Being Yourself: How to Lose Your Mind and Create a New One.* He talks about breaking out of the comfort zone and overcoming the resistance that keeps us stuck in the same place. He says, "If you want a new outcome, you will have to break the habit of being yourself, and reinvent a new self." How many people know this is even possible?

Turns out if you want prosperity, well being and a totally emotionally rich life, you have to understand where your Resistance is coming from, increase your level of Dissatisfaction with your current situation, create a strong and powerful Vision and be willing to take decisive First Steps. The following story will demonstrate the Formula for Change through my personal experience *going big* and stepping out of my comfort zone in my college days.

My Vision Was Ignited in the Wild, Wild West

My first trip out West via Interstate 70 from Dayton, Ohio direct to Denver, Colorado was truly life changing. Just after my freshman year at college I received an invitation from two friends to "head west" for a fabulous 2-week adventure. I said, "YES!" and off we went on a non-stop road trip with one destination on our minds — *The Rocky Mountains*. Seeing the looming layers of snow-capped mountains in the distance as we drew closer and closer across the Colorado plains filled me with excitement like I had never known. The image was surreal. Mountains existed for me in the movies and on TV, but this was my first exposure to the real deal "up close and in person". I could hardly believe my eyes!

Once we arrived and met up with a friend who was a Denver local, we did everything possible to experience the area in fine fashion. We rock climbed and repelled, camped out, hiked several hours up a big mountain, drove through the rock canyons outside of Boulder, and hiked around Rocky Mountain National Park. The experience literally *took my breath away*. I was absolutely smitten with the mountains and phenomenal landscape, and soon found myself wondering how I could live in these magnificent mountains. By the time I arrived back at *Bowling Green State University* two weeks later, I was committed to finding a way to make this happen.

First Steps & Massive Action to Make it Happen and Move West

We have all heard the saying "where there is a will, there is a way". When the timing is right, this works. The vision I had of the mountain lifestyle was fresh in my mind and heart. As I started to talk to my college friends about my dream, I quickly discovered a girl in my dorm that shared my vision and also had her heart set on moving west. She had many friends who visited and she was ready to make the leap. In the cafeteria we made a pact we would find a way to move west together — despite the fact our parents were financing our schooling and we had no money of our own to make this dream happen. *Minor detail*. We were committed to our now collective vision and nothing would stop us.

Want It Badly Enough And It Will Become a *Magnificent Obsession*

I became obsessed with moving west and nothing was going to stop me from realizing this big dream. The power and intensity and duration of this desire became non-stop. The REPETITION of thought and IMAGES of what my life in the mountains would be ignited the power of the "Law of Creation". I spoke about it to everyone (SOUND), and felt fantastic (EMOTION) when I thought about my dream.

Within a week I found out about a National Student Exchange program where we could go to school in a different state and our parents would still pay in-state tuition to Bowling Green State University, our local college. The first step was to convince both our parents this was a great idea. Seeing as we were both quite persuasive, we easily tackled that hurdle. Our parents felt this would be a wonderful life experience and fully believed we would be back after the exchange year . . .

I headed to the college library and researched climates and locations from the list of universities out west, which did not include Colorado. We submitted our list and within a short time were accepted at Montana State University in Bozeman, Montana. *Woo-hoo, we were on our way west!*

Once there, I finished college at Montana State University and ended up living in the *Wild, Wild West* of Montana for over 20 years. I was sorry to be so far from my family, yet it was truly a dream come true to live the magical mountain lifestyle I had envisioned on that first trip to Colorado. I learned to ski, hunt, camp and hiked to the top of many mountains. I mountain biked all over creation, and enjoyed "hot potting" in the numerous hot springs surrounding Yellowstone Park. I became an entrepreneur there delivering business training seminars and motivational speeches. Before that I sold western art and even owned a bar and grille in the remote Madison Valley of Montana, *The Grizzly Bar*. I loved the mountain lifestyle and lived a life most people only dream about or see in the movies — absolutely fantastic.

"You are today where your thoughts have brought you, you will be tomorrow where your thoughts take you." — James Allen

Events, Circumstances and People Will Be Drawn to You like Magic

When you have a vision, and think about it over and over with power and intensity; the events, circumstance and people you need to make it happen will be drawn to you like magic. Before I even knew about the "Law of Creation", this experience was just one example of putting the **RISE to Success** principles in action and reaping the rewards in my life.

I can honestly say my move west to Montana was a beginning for me to achieve something super-big in my life that I really wanted. It felt *fantastic*. I was crystal clear that I wanted to move west, and that is the absolute first step — *know what you want*. Now it is your turn. Decide exactly what you want and use the **RISE to Success System** to bring it into reality:

> REPETITION - Think about what you want over and over.
> IMAGES - See a vision of what it is you want.
> SOUND - Talk about it and declare the positive outcome.
> EMOTION - Feel really good when you see it happening.

Time to Score Your Likelihood for Change Using the Formula

Let's pull this together so you can apply the formula in your own life and business and evaluate the likelihood for you to make any change you want or need to have happen. Each section of the formula will be rated on a scale of 1-10.

VISION - While in Colorado, I imagined living the mountain lifestyle due to the phenomenal experiences I had over those two weeks. I made a *decision* to find a way to live out west all the time. As the saying goes "where there is a will there is a way" and my *Wild West* Story perfectly aligned with this. My vision was strong and my passion for all that awaited me on a daily basis was a 10.

Score: 10

DISSATISFACTION - I really did not know how dissatisfied I was with life in Ohio until I came west and experienced a very different landscape and the alluring adventurous lifestyle that I savored with every breath and step I took. At that point I realized I wanted more. On a scale of 1-10, my dissatisfaction with my current life in the flatlands of Ohio became a 10.

> **TIP**
> Dissatisfaction is often the biggest key to bring about life change

Score: 10

FIRST STEPS - The first steps I took to achieve my dream was to attract and partner with someone who shared my same vision. The law of attraction connected us and also led us to the National Student Exchange program. Other first steps were to get approval from my parents as well as research the exchange schools and pick the ones to which I would apply. On a scale of 1-10, I took massive and immediate action at a level 10.

Score: 10

RESISTANCE - In my case I was looking toward the change as something fun and exciting, had no fear and completely believed it was possible. My parents, who were financing my vision, could have been the ones to come up with some resistance, but fortunately they did not. They were totally on board, as were the college advisors, all of who believed it would be a great growth experience for me as a college junior. On a scale of 1-10, I had zero resistance.

Score: 0

What Did The Change Formula Reveal About My Likelihood to Change?

This Formula for Change requires some basic math, which will deliver a score for how likely it is change will be made in your life. Each situation will be different. The Formula for Change never lies, however, and will help you to see what may hold you back from making any change you really want. Here are our formula results:

$$(V \times D) + F > R$$

1. Insert my scores into the formula: [V (10) X D (10)] + F (10) > R (0)
2. Begin to do the math: [100] + (10) = 110 > 0
3. Check out the left side and the right side and see which is greater: 110 > 0
4. If the left side is greater than the right, change is likely . . .
5. If the right side is greater than the left, change is unlikely . . .

In my case study the left side was 110 and the right side was zero! Change was eminent. Now you see why the change we both wanted to see in our world actually happened. This fun *Wild, Wild West* story showcases *the best-case scenario*, with the highest and best numbers possible in each category of the Formula for Change. Even if in your situation your numbers are lower than this story portrays, the left side just has to be greater than the right.

For instance, there was the stay-at-home-mom who returned to the workforce from Chapter 3: "SOUND: You Will Have What You Say! The Power of Words" Nancy had been out of the workplace for over twenty years and was unhappy with this situation now that her children were grown (Dissatisfaction). She really wanted a job (Vision) but was not that confident it could happen. Recently, with the help of mentors, she shifted her paradigm by adopting a new belief in her talents and abilities (First Steps). She overcame her past and was empowered to rise above her previous negative identity (Resistance). She reinforced her positive qualities, and landed a job based on what she was now saying and believing about herself. She is successful and happy in her job. *This was a big life change*. Here are her numbers in the Formula for Change:

[VISION (3) x DISSATISFACTION (7)] = 21 + FIRST STEPS (5) = 26 > RESISTANCE (6). 26 is greater than 6. Change is likely . . .

In another scenario we have a battered wife of a very successful businessman who buys her jewels and high-end cars and keeps her in a lifestyle of luxury. Her vision of a life on her own is totally out of her mindset, even though there is a slight glimmer occasionally. She has no skills, no family to turn to, she loves him and just can't imagine life without him, even though the abuse is tough and hurts. She has made a couple calls and one visit to the battered women's resource center, but she felt terribly guilty and decided she would never do that again. Let's run the numbers:

[VISION (1) x DISSATISFACTION (4)] = 4 + FIRST STEPS (1) = 5 > RESISTANCE (10). 5 is less than 10. Change is unlikely . . .

You alone will be able to analyze where you stand in this formula, and how ready you are to make a change in your life. Your ability to make positive changes in each specific area of the formula will determine what level of success you experience. To bring about change:

1. Increase your VISION of your ideal future.
2. Increase your level of DISSATISFACTION with your current reality.
3. Ramp up the action level in your FIRST STEPS.
4. Overcome the RESISTANCE that holds you back.

You must want something different or better in your life in order for the **RISE to Success** process to work. You have to be ready, willing and able to change your reality. Are you ready to think, feel, and act in new ways? Are you ready to become someone else? Are you ready to be proactive instead of reactive in life? Are you ready to envision a brighter future? Are you ready to change environments, both internal and external? If you answered "YES", then let's go!

Walt Disney Used the Formula for Change to Create His Disney Dynasty

Let's review how the Formula for Change was securely in place to create *Walt Disney World* from Chapter One:

VISION - Disney dreamed of a much larger theme park with many more attractions for children and families to enjoy and discover.

DISSATISFACTION - He did not like being hemmed in by the land constraints of the city of Los Angeles as *Disneyland* was.

FIRST STEPS - Walt began buying parcel by parcel of land in Florida in secret, and inspired his brother and the *Disney* organization to get on board with his dream.

RESISTANCE - He had no fear or negative thoughts to prevent him from more business development. He had no limiting beliefs. He overcame any outside resistance with persistence and positive energy to stay the course. There was no force that could have held him back from achieving the greatness of the world's largest theme park.

Outcome: His score on the left side was *much higher* than his score on the right. Change was inevitable for Walt Disney in his creation of a new them park.

―――――――――

WHY YOU LEARNED IN CHAPTER 6:
Easy Math Formula Predicts Your Likelihood to Change

In order to bring about CHANGE in your life, you must know what you want in your heart (Vision), clarify your level of unhappiness with your current reality (Dissatisfaction) and take immediate action to bring about the change (First Steps). All of this must add up to a number greater than what is on the other side of the math formula, which can keep it from happening (Resistance).

- Formula for Change is (V x D) + F > R
  - Rate Vision on a scale of 1-10
  - Rate Dissatisfaction on a scale of 1-10
  - Rate First Steps on a scale of 1-10
  - Rate Resistance on a scale of 1-10
- Evaluate your personal situation and enter the numbers in the formula
- If the left side is greater than the right, change is likely
- If the right side is great than the left, change is unlikely

Much of life operates within this easy math formula, and now you can use this to your advantage to strategize your change process. Once you know your numbers, you can implement the **RISE to Success** system to bring about the positive results that you want in all areas of your life.

Demystify Beliefs to Improve Health, Wealth & Happiness

7

As a veteran in the field of personal and professional development I have heard beliefs spoken about thousands of times. Funny thing is, it wasn't until I started writing this book that I realized I wasn't sure how a belief is actually formed. I knew the impact they have on our lives - the way our beliefs determine our health, our wealth and multitudes of outcomes in our lives. But how are they created . . . really?

Let's just get right to the point and de-mystify beliefs and how they are formed. Check out the following equation and drawing and you will see how it happens:

Dominant and Repetitive Thoughts Create Your Beliefs

Thought + thought + thought + focused attention + thought + thought + thought + focused energy = dominant thought + thought + thought + stronger vibration + thought + thought + thought + higher frequency + thought + thought + thought + longer duration + thought + thought + thought = BELIEF = life experience.

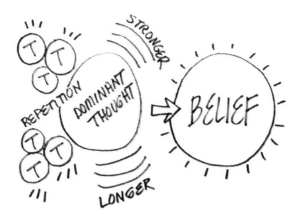

Beliefs are a much bigger, bolder collection of ingrained thoughts. Did you notice the very first step of the formula is based on a REPETITION of thoughts? As mentioned earlier, the thoughts we think over and over are the ones that impact our life. You will hear this reinforced throughout the book.

> "You are a living magnet. What you attract into your life is in harmony with your dominant thoughts."
> — Brian Tracy, Author and Speaker

How miraculous that we can shape our own beliefs with habitual patterns of thought. It is up to us! We are in the driver's seat and we can choose negative, neutral or positive. Positive, empowering beliefs are the highway to a happy, healthy life.

How can you be sure of what you currently believe right now? The first clue is to look at your life and observe your current reality:

- Where are you living?
- Do you feel happy and joyful?
- Who are your friends?
- Is your business making money?
- How is your health?
- Do you feel fulfilled?

Our Early Years Have a Big Impact on Brain Wiring

Especially during our "formative years" of childhood, up to 7 or 8 years of age, we acquire countless cellular memories and experiences that shape who we are today. Most of those memories are buried deep in our subconscious, and we cannot even recall them. We made choices about things that were said or done to us, which created an identity of who we are.

Have you ever wondered why two children can grow up in the same household and have very different personalities? For example, take my two sisters and me — *we are all so different*. My youngest sister is a high performing executive with a stable home life, close friends, and a husband and children who adore her. The other sister is a mentally troubled victim who is estranged from all extended family, and lives a reclusive life on a remote island. And then there's me... somewhere in the middle!

My dysfunctional sister and I both had some very tough and exceedingly damaging childhood experiences that my other sister did not have. We also had the same parents, and my high performing sister had a different Dad.

If it wasn't for my career in personal and professional development, I have no idea where I would be today. Over the years I learned to take responsibility for my life, and to make it better. I read and studied diligently and sought mentors and teachers and helpers throughout my life. I was always ready and willing to work on myself until I had breakthroughs. And I applied the principles I am teaching in this book which have changed my life, too. That is why I get so excited about sharing all I have learned about the brain, body, mind, and spirit with you.

Each one of us chooses millions of times throughout our lives how we interpret reality and the *story* of who we are. "You are smart", "you are pretty", "you are lazy", "you are creative", "you are a pain" or "you don't deserve it". Can you think about your parents, grandparents, great-grandparents, teachers, doctors, coaches, and community leaders who programmed you to believe you were either powerless or powerful? In my own family, I received conflicting messages of my value and self-worth:

- My stepfather who raised me from age three, told me calmly and assuredly as a teenager, "Patrice, you have what it takes to be a successful businesswoman." This built up my self-confidence and is very much the reason why I have had the courage to be an entrepreneur my entire adult life. He recognized my natural talent and believed in me.
- My mother loved me deeply, but she unknowingly took all her unresolved anger and resentment towards my birth father out on me. She would fly off the handle and say, "You're sick, you're just like your father — you need a psychiatrist!" If I heard that pet phrase of hers once, I heard it 300 times. It was like a knife stabbing me in the heart. I felt terrible and ashamed of myself.

As I listened to both statements repetitively, they went into my subconscious mind and made an impact on my beliefs and identity. One was positive and empowering; the other was hurtful and deflating. I am sure you have your own subconscious programming from experiences from your youth. What sticks in your mind as some of the frequent statements you heard that shaped your beliefs?

A favorite writer and speaker of mine, the late Wayne Dyer, wrote a book with a very unique title. We have all heard the saying "I'll believe it when I see it" to describe the doubt we can have to receive a relationship, a contract, a new job, or anything we really want. We want it proven to us before we really believe. In Dyer's book the title is opposite: *I Will See it When I Believe it.* His book is based on the premise that the belief *must* come first. Once you truly believe, then your desires will appear.

As you reflect over time, you may realize that many of the beliefs that propel your life are false and self-limiting. I hope you will be inspired to change those beliefs with the **RISE to Success** system. This process is powerful — *I know it is*. The life I have created using these techniques is a much richer and satisfying one. And I, too, am still in process of "overcoming" and *rising above* the limitations of my past.

This work is a deeper process for some than others; it certainly has been a challenging one for me.

4 Ways To Strengthen Your Belief in Yourself

Following are some unique stories and examples to illustrate four ways to override limiting beliefs:

1. **Hyper-Focus On Success**
2. **Be More Than Your Environment**
3. **Think Really BIG!**
4. **Be Inspired By Your Hero**

1. Hyper-Focus On Success

Focusing on success conditions your mind to believe in your success. Focusing on failure does the exact opposite. Thoughts of failure condition the mind to think other thoughts that produce more failure. As you let the master thought "I will succeed" dominate your thought process, remarkable things will happen. The strength of your vision combined with your success belief will seal the deal. Here is Jim Carrey's story:

Jim Carrey Visualizes Movie Star Fame atop Mulholland Drive, Hollywood

Jim Carrey tells his story of being a comic trying to make it into Hollywood movies around 1990. He actually drove to the top of Mulholland Drive and looked down on the city below and imagined a successful future. He would stretch out his arm and say, *"Everyone wants to work with me. I'm a really good actor. I have all kinds of great movie offers."* He said he would repeat it over and over to convince himself it was true.

Carrey also wrote himself a $10 million dollar check for "acting services rendered" and carried it in his wallet and looked at it every day. By Thanksgiving 1995, the date on his check, Jim Carrey was already an established comedic actor with movies like *Dumb & Dumber, Ace Ventura: Pet Detective* and *The Mask*, commanding up to $20 million per picture.

This is an incredible story of the **RISE to Success** system at work with REPETITION of thoughts, IMAGES, SOUND and EMOTION to achieve a very specific super-sized goal.

2. Be More Than Your Environment

Did you start out in a rough neighborhood, with a father who beat you, or were you abandoned by your parents as a baby? Did you have abusive parents or an oppressive upbringing? There are people in this world who have had modest or even terrible beginnings in life, but they rose above their circumstances and became successful. This requires being proactive and believing you can be more than your humble beginnings, your hurtful past, and even your current reality. One famous person from humble beginnings, who believed in herself and imagined more, is Oprah Winfrey. Here is her story:

Oprah's Childhood Moment of Inspiration Set the Course for Her Future

Oprah's grandmother was a housekeeper. Oprah said she remembers watching her hang clothes on the line on a very still, very quiet day at their home in the country. Her grandmother wanted her to watch closely, and said *"Someday you will have to learn how to do this yourself"*. Oprah was 4-5 years old and in that memorable instant a belief welled up in her that there was much more for her life than being a housekeeper. She said she could feel it, she knew it in her soul and she imagined more for herself, even though she did not see the details at the time.

We all know how successful Oprah has been as a media icon: someone who influences culture, interviews people and is known for her heart-to-heart communication. How heartwarming to know her vision for something better at such a young age sparked an empowering belief. That belief positively impacted her life and millions of others.

3. Think Really Big!

Believe success has your name on it. The size of your success is determined by the size of your belief. Think little goals and expect little achievements. Think big goals and win big success. Remind yourself regularly that you are better than you think you are. Successful people are not superhuman, just regular people who have developed belief in themselves and what they do. Never — yes, *never* — sell yourself short. A current successful National Football League (NFL) player shares how the power of belief was instilled in him at a very young age:

Dad Challenges Sports-minded Son, Russell Wilson, "Why Not You?"

One of my favorite NFL football players is the Seattle Seahawk's quarterback Russell Wilson. He shares with everyone the words his father said constantly to him, "Russell, why not you? You can be a championship ball player. You can be super successful. Someone is going to be, *why not you*?" These words super-charged Russell's belief system (subconscious mind). Along with his dad getting him up every day at 5:00 am to practice and train, he went on to fulfill the positive declarations spoken to him.

When the Seahawks called to notify him he had been drafted, he told them with great confidence it was the best decision they ever made! In his second year in the NFL, he led the Seahawks to a Super Bowl 48 win. Wilson secured a 4-year $87 million contract with $60 million guaranteed. He started the *Why Not You Foundation* to help youth in the Seattle area to believe in themselves, become leaders and do great things. Now those are positive results from a brain wired for success to *think really BIG!*

4. Be Inspired By Your Hero

Who are your heroes? It could be someone you know personally like a neighbor or a teacher. Your hero could be a world leader, movie hero, or sports figure. It could even be a child who inspires you. When a challenge comes up in your life, imagine this person dealing with a situation "heroically." What would it be like to be in their shoes? How can you transfer their positive qualities to yourself? This is exactly what I do with one of my heroes, Louise Hay. Hay was a "late bloomer" in the impact of her legacy, which I find quite moving. Whenever I start to place limits on myself due to my age, I think of her and her youthful determinism:

Louise Hay Busts Through Age Barriers in her 60's, 70's, and 80's

Very vocal in her belief that age was irrelevant to achieving one's dreams, at 81, Louise Hay released her first-ever film on her life and work, *You Can Heal Your Life: The Movie.* She published her book, *You Can Heal Your Life*, just shy of age 60. In it, Louise explains how our beliefs and ideas about ourselves are often the cause of our emotional problems and physical maladies and how, by using certain tools, we can change our thinking and our lives for the better. *You Can Heal Your Life* became a *New York Times* bestseller and spent 16 weeks on the list. More than 50 million copies of *You Can Heal Your Life* have been sold worldwide. Louise Hay passed away while I was writing this book at age 90.

You are a product of your own thoughts when they are repeated fre-quently enough to become beliefs. Believe *big*. Implement the **RISE to Success** system to develop powerful habits filled with sincere, honest beliefs that you can succeed. This growing collection of habits will shape your paradigms. When you change your paradigm programs, you change your life. Your behaviors flow from your paradigms and beliefs. And your results flow from your habits and behaviors. Believe *big* and live *big*!

Our Dominant Beliefs Influence Our Health More Than Our Genes

As we have uncovered, a belief is not "the gospel"; it is simply a repeated thought pattern that is etched into your subconscious mind through habit. We think a thought over and over and over until it pops from a dominant thought into a *belief*. I want to share with you some cutting edge science that explains how our beliefs actually impact us at a cellular level — *in the brains of our cells*.

When I attended a *Law of Attraction Meetup* in Dayton, Ohio a fellow participant shared an interesting tidbit. She explained that everyone in her group at work was enrolled in genetic tests so they could find out what genetic markers they have for certain diseases. I had to speak up and interrupt this belief pattern that reinforced the power of genetic determinism on our health. By nature, the *Meetup* group is made up of people open to the idea that we create our reality in many ways, including our thoughts. This gave me the opening to speak up.

"Have you heard of *The Biology of Belief* by Bruce Lipton?" I asked the group. I was surprised that no one had. I explained how this book changed my life by giving me the science to explain how our beliefs determine our health more than genes ever could. I shared that Dr. Bruce Lipton, PhD is a medical doctor who also taught doctors at the University of Wisconsin and Stanford, in addition to being a researcher.

He conducted some landmark experiments with cells and discovered the brain of the cell is *not* in the nucleus where the DNA resides, but in the cell membrane. He came to this conclusion when he removed the nucleus of the cell and it still lived and functioned as a living organism. To relate on a human level, if we removed our brains from our skulls, we would not be functioning; we would be dead! But the cells in his experiment did not die; they were very much alive.

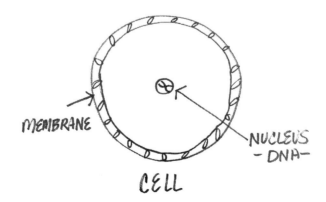

The Cell Membrane Is the Brain of Our Cells, Not The Nucleus

I was spellbound to hear Bruce Lipton share his discovery that the brain of the cell is not in the DNA at the center or nucleus of the cell, as many believe. The cell's brain is located in its cell membrane, encircling the cell on the outside edge. Dr. Lipton went on to conclude that the **environment** in which the cell lived affected the cell brain the most. Among other items like food and liquid, the single and most surprising item that influences the cell membrane the most are our *beliefs*! This blew my mind. Why is this message not being yelled from every rooftop across the country? *This is very exciting indeed.* Our beliefs do determine our health and our lives to a much greater extent than the average person realizes.

The New Biology and the Link to Our Beliefs

Dr. Bruce Lipton, PhD ended up leaving his second medical school, Stanford, and writing *The Biology of Belief* in an attempt to get this word out to the masses of people like you and me. He knew we needed to hear and understand these facts so we can take control of our own lives, health, and destiny! Dr. Lipton revealed that even though his discoveries could have rocked the world of biology, none of his colleagues were even interested in his research because they were so steeped into the outdated theory (yes, *theory*) of Newtonian physics, the basis of genetic determinism.

> "It takes an old theory years or even decades to get out of the general mindset even when it doesn't fit anymore."
> — Dr. Ben Johnson, *The Healing Code*

The establishment doctors' long held beliefs were comfortable to them and therefore to the biologists and medical students they influenced and trained. Remember the section on *Resistance* in Chapter 6: "Easy Math Formula Predicts Your Likelihood to Change"? The comfort zone has a powerful hold on people. Most of the medical community is stuck in "this is the way it has always been", the traditional *cause and effect paradigm* of Newtonian physics.

Along with this old physics model is the belief that our DNA decides our destiny on a cellular level. So if you have a gene for cancer, you are predisposed to cancer. If you have a gene for blue eyes you will likely have blue eyes. If you have a gene for baldness, you will eventually be bald. If you have a gene for Alzheimer's, you will likely get Alzheimer's. And so on.

In our society today this is still an accepted theory. Remember the news story about famous actress Angelina Jolie? She had both her breasts removed because her aunt and sister had contracted breast cancer and she had the same cancer gene as they did. This is a perfect example of a powerful paradigm that has a grip on most people. And now you know the truth, so maybe you will reconsider, and decide you don't have to be among that group of people.

> "We are living in exciting times, for science is in the process of shattering old myths and rewriting a fundamental belief of human civilization. The belief that we are frail biochemical machines controlled by genes is giving way to an understanding that we are powerful creators of our lives and the world we live in." — Bruce H. Lipton PhD, Author of *The Biology of Belief*

Epigenetics — Environment Rules Over Genetics

Today one of the most active areas of scientific research is epigenetics: the study of the molecular mechanisms by which environment controls gene activity. This field of biology is unraveling the mysteries of how the environment (nature) influences the behavior of cells without changing the genetic code.

Back at the *Law of Attraction Meetup*, I reassured the woman who was excited about her genetic test results. I said, "Please tell your colleagues, and know yourself that the results of these tests are only predispositions based on old, outdated science. Please do not let the genetic results into your heart and mind as stone, cold facts. Know that your own personal beliefs and lifestyle habits are much more influential and important to your health than your genes."

Okay, I did my part to get this important message out to the world by operating in my sphere of influence at that meeting and by writing this book. My hope is that you will share this message with your sphere of influence as well, and together we can help stop the madness and dependence on the traditional medical system as the final word on our health.

We have established in this chapter that Newtonian physics is responsible for the theory of genetic determinism, also known as the law of cause and effect. Let's introduce quantum physics as the science of energy and subatomic particles, and as you will learn later, is based on the premise that we can cause an effect. We truly do have much more ability to impact our health and wealth than we have been led to believe. In Chapter 13: "Quantum Physics Doesn't Have to Be Hard — Here's Why", we will delve into this deeply.

It is truly my passion to share this valuable, life-giving knowledge with you. How exhilarating is it to know we can change the character of our lives, our bodies, our minds, by changing our beliefs! We can be co-creators of our destiny. As we become more informed about the science behind **RISE to Success,** we can move beyond a victim mentality and create lives overflowing with peace, happiness, and love.

Our beliefs do control our lives and here is the good news — *we can control our beliefs*. They are just ideas we can change, not absolute truths. Through repetition of thought, mental imagery, sound declarations and positive emotions, our lives can change significantly to become what we imagine them to be.

What You Learned in Chapter 7:
Demystify Beliefs to Improve Health, Wealth & Happiness

Beliefs are powerful. Our beliefs and paradigms determine our results in life. The truth of how beliefs are formed is simpler than you might have imagined.

- Dominant, and repetitive thoughts with energy create your beliefs.
- Our early years have a big impact on brain wiring. Comments we heard over and over shaped our future identity — our habits of thinking and feeling and behaving.
- Cell membrane is the brain of our cells, not nucleus where DNA resides.
- Our beliefs are more powerful than our genes.
- Epigenetics – the scientific study of how environment rules over genetics.
- We live in a medical model paradigm shift most people have no clue about.
- Newtonian physics of genetic determinism is the law of cause and effect.
- Quantum physics is based on energy and us being able to cause an effect.

We can choose to strengthen our belief in ourselves with these strategies:

1. Hyper-Focus On Success
2. Be More Than Your Environment
3. Think Really BIG!
4. Be Inspired By Your Hero

It is your time to take these strategies and run with them to create health and wellbeing beyond what you could ask, hope or imagine. *I believe in you*.

8 Your Subconscious Super Robot is in Charge of Your Life

As we discussed in the previous chapter, our beliefs are ingrained deeply into our subconscious mind. In this chapter, you will learn about the interplay between the conscious and subconscious minds. You will discover the limits of your conscious mind and the incredible power of your subconscious. The internal resistance to achieve your personal vision is a very real force you will want to overcome. Basically, it is time to *let the force be with you*, not against you.

Conscious and Subconscious Minds are Interdependent

At this point, we have all heard about the conscious and subconscious mind. Let's review what we may know. Later we will add some facts to open our eyes even more to the impact the subconscious mind has on us. I will use the more common term "subconscious" to represent anything beneath the surface of our conscious mind. This includes the "unconscious" (automatic body programs) and what some refer to as the "nonconscious" (unconscious + subconscious).

Conscious Mind

The conscious mind is the part of us that can conjure up positive thoughts, vision, and goals through reasoning, intellect, and free will. It is creative and imaginative. As it relates to our **RISE to Success** process, the conscious mind allows us to make clear and present choices about what we want, think, see, say, and feel.

Subconscious Mind

Our subconscious mind is typically filled with things like beliefs, perceptions, memory pictures, and learned experiences. This is where triggers from the past, instinctive reactions, and stimulus/response programming are found. Our subconscious contains a lifetime of habits of thinking, feeling, and being based on our unique maps of reality.

These two minds interrelate and affect each other. By itself, conscious positive thinking cannot overcome the negative programming and feelings of our subconscious mind. By the time we reach midlife, much of our behavior is on autopilot. Our subconscious programs determine how we shower, eat breakfast, drive to work, react to stress, etc. On the negative emotional side we have ingrained habits to: get frustrated in traffic, worry about the future, judge people, hyper focus on faults, and grow angry over nuisances.

A targeted effort to reprogram your subconscious is the only way the positive can override the negative that exists beneath the surface. **RISE to Success** is a powerful daily strategy to help you accomplish this objective.

Subconscious Mind is the Mass of the Iceberg You Can't See

To make this clear in your mind, imagine an iceberg with its tip being your conscious mind and the mass beneath the surface as your subconscious. If you remember the story, it was the hidden mass of the iceberg that sunk the famous *Titanic* ocean liner. The same can be true for you and the fate of your visions and goals. Resistance operating beneath the surface can stop you cold. You can, however, make the necessary course corrections to avoid obstacles and reach your freedom destination.

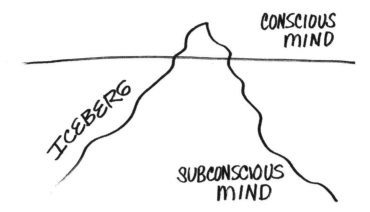

Any conflict between your conscious and subconscious mind can impede progress. It is mission critical for you to know that when these two forces are at war, the subconscious wins every time! It's like the missile (subconscious) versus the water pistol (conscious) when it comes to weapons. Can you see how it is a good idea not to underestimate the phenomenal power of your subconscious mind?

Alex Loyd in his groundbreaking book, *The Healing Code*, describes the conscious as the "Head" and the nonconscious auto programming as the "Heart". He also says, "When the head and heart conflict, the heart wins every time". This is another way to identify the internal battle many of us have — granted, some more than others.

Facts About the Subconscious and Conscious Mind

As I mentioned in the introduction, John Assaraf's book appeared to jump off the shelf and into my hands when I stopped in an airport gift shop. His research has greatly impacted my understanding of the brain and mind. The following chart is reprinted with permission from Assaraf's book *You Can Have it All*. What an excellent way to visually and logically learn how much more power your subconscious (nonconscious as he calls it) has over your conscious mind. Take a moment to let this sink in.

	Conscious	Nonconscious
Brain Mass	17%	83%
Speed of impulse	124-140 mph	Over 100,000 mph
Bits/second	2,000	400 billion
Control of perception and behavior	2-4%	90-98%
Function	Volitional	Servile
Time	Past and future	Present
Memory horizon	Up to 20 seconds	Forever

Your Subconscious Performs Like a Super Robot

What conclusions can you draw from this chart? It appears to me that our subconscious (nonconscious on the chart) is like a super robotic character — way bigger, way faster, and way more in control than a mere mortal. Always ready to serve its master (us), the super robot is present focused and never forgets anything. Haven't you ever wanted to have your own personal robot on call day and night? Now you do. It's your subconscious mind. Are you game to learn how to operate your robot, and get it working with you to design an extraordinary life?

SUBCONSCIOUS SUPER ROBOT

Once your subconscious knows what you want, it will use its massive super power go to work for you. *You just need to tell it exactly what you want.* If you program the subconscious well, it will direct you efficiently and effectively to your destination. This is more than your conscious mind could ever do, because the conscious mind is not powerful enough to compute the data. Your brain is like a computer, and the subconscious works at 100,000 miles per hour and processes 400 billion bits per second (versus 2,000). It also *loves to serve you*.

If you watched the movie *The Secret*, you saw how Jack Canfield used his subconscious to manifest a $100,000 yearly income goal. He took a $1 bill and wrote zeros on it to make it $100,000. He taped the money on his ceiling above his bed. Every morning and night, he looked at the bill and imagined he would achieve the goal. Canfield programmed his subconscious mind two times per day, and it went to work for him day and night. At the end of the year, he had earned $92,000, much more than he ever had previously. He went on eventually to use this strategy for a million. And that worked, too.

We have established the dynamic between your conscious and subconscious. Let's look at another way to *let the force be with you*, not against you to get the results you want.

Two Opposing Forces Determine If You Reach Your Vision

In the diagram below, the lower solid line represents your "Current Reality"; where you are now in life. The higher line on the diagram represents your "Vision" of your life; where you want to be. Your vision could include more money, better health, richer relationships, and more passionate work — all of the dreams you hold for your future.

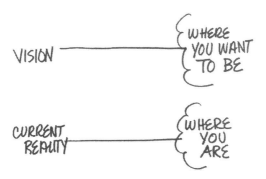

There are pressures being exerted both ways: *driving forces* to move the "Current Reality" line up towards your "Vision" and *restraining forces* exerting pressure on the "Vision" line to push it down toward your "Current Reality". The goal of the restraining forces is to keep you trapped right where you are. Remember the tendency for many people to stay in their comfort zone and not change? These forces can be external or internal. For the purpose of this chapter, we will focus on the internal.

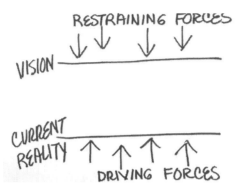

Examples of Internal Driving Forces

- Vision /mission/ goals
- Inspired effort and action
- Rituals/Discipline
- Positive thoughts and feelings
- Dissatisfaction with current reality
- Creativity/Imagination

Examples of Internal Restraining Forces

- Limiting beliefs/Incorrect paradigms
- Destructive cellular memories and unhealed trauma
- Low level emotions: fear, anxiety, doubt, worry, depression
- Negative memory pictures on your Image-screen
- Poor self-identity
- Excuses and procrastination

Resistance Holds You Back From Your Vision

In the stories of the *Wild, Wild West* and *Disney World* earlier in the book, we introduced the concept of *Resistance* as the limiting element in the Formula for Change. Restraining forces can keep you back from positive change and the life you desire. Your *Dissatisfaction*, *Vision* and *First Steps* are driving forces to propel you forward and override the annoying restraining forces.

You may not have control over funding, decisions of the board, mortgage crisis, recession, hurricanes, car problems, or a parent who says, "No". These are all outside forces. The inside restraining forces listed above are the ones over which you do have control. Unfortunately, you may not be aware these forces are at work against you — because they exist *beyond your conscious awareness*. They are found in the mass of the iceberg.

This is a tough situation, actually. It's not entirely fair because, in general, no one in your life previously offered you this explanation. You might have discovered it on your own, as I did. To save you time and money, I am here now as your trusty guide. I will enlighten you about these forces, the control you have over them, and help you rise above them.

Techniques to Reprogram the Body-Mind-Spirit and Overcome Resistance Forces

Are you ready to reprogram your subconscious restraining forces and be released to succeed? The **RISE to Success** system provides a super succinct and powerful technique. Let's take a look at how **RISE** can reprogram the restraining forces in your subconscious mind.

New beliefs are formed by repetitive patterns of focused attention; as you think, write, speak, and envision what you truly want, you reprogram your inner identity. Daily practice of positive thoughts and elevated emotion will create new pathways and override previous subconscious programming. Daily entries into your **RISE to Success Journal** will impress into your psyche the life you want to live. A weak thought becomes stronger and stronger when you intentionally think it over time, day after day, week after week. Eventually, change will occur, and the magic will happen.

Depending on many variables, you may need to incorporate additional practices to the system to eliminate deep blocks in your subconscious mind from early life programming or past traumatic events. Here are a few more of my personal secret strategies I want to share with you:

1. Energy healing methods
2. Inner healing prayer
3. Activation energy techniques
4. Meditation audio programs
5. Reprogramming statements

Energy healing methods: Ones I personally know to be excellent are *The Healing Code, The Emotion Code, Emotional Freedom Technique* (also called tapping or EFT), *Bioenergetic synchronization technique* (*BEST)* and *Theta Healing*. The Healing Code, which drastically changed my life, uses quantum mechanics to accomplish the healing. Bad "human hard drive" programming is targeted and healed with these simple techniques. This negative energy programming originates from destructive cellular memories, unhealthy beliefs and harmful memory pictures.

Inner healing prayer: This procedure is based on the book *Transformation of the Inner Man,* written by John Sandford. Hallmarks of the program are elimination of bitterroot judgments and inner lies, birthed in the past. When they are identified and released, life-changing freedom is restored to the individuals.

Activation energy techniques: A starting ritual is a repeated behavior adopted in order to activate a new behavior. The book *The 5 Second Rule* by Mel Robbins uses this technique. *The 5 Second Rule* is quite effective to eliminate restraining forces like procrastination, excuses, low level emotions and poor identity. Robbins says, "The moment you have an instinct to act on a goal you must physically move within 5 seconds or your brain will stop you. 5-4-3-2-1-GO!" **RISE to Success** morning ritual is also an activation energy technique.

Meditation audio programs: Consistent meditation will allow you to access the subconscious and reprogram it for health, wealth, and happiness. These programs are so much more than a relaxation style of meditation. Some of my favorite creators in this arena are Dr. Joe Dispenza, Jack Canfield and Jon Assaraf. They all have a variety of guided meditations proven to facilitate internal shifts.

Reprogramming statements: Based on over twenty years as a PhD psychotherapist, Dr. Alex Loyd created this list of statements. He says they are designed to deprogram our mind and heart back into the perfect state they were in when our human hard drives were virus free. These statements are a simple procedure you can use to deprogram and reprogram yourself. Please refer to the reference section for further details on Loyd's books.

Because there is so much more to say about the reprogramming process, I am inspired to share more of what I know with you. This will be the subject of my emails, social media posts and forthcoming books. So, stay tuned.

What You Learned in Chapter 8:
Your Subconscious Super Robot is in Charge of Your Life

Our beliefs do control our lives. But what is the good news? *We can control our beliefs.* Even though our subconscious mind is much more powerful and in control than our conscious mind, we can use our conscious mind to change our subconscious programming.

- Our conscious and subconscious minds are interdependent. The conscious mind conjures up positive thoughts, vision, and goals through reasoning, intellect and free will.
- The subconscious is made of beliefs, perceptions, memory pictures, and learned experiences that shape our paradigms.
- Our subconscious is like a "Super Robot" that works *for us* day and night.
- Habits are made of repetitive behaviors that happen automatically over time.

- Driving forces work to propel us toward our vision. Restraining forces work to keep us back from achieving our vision.
- There are a multitude of techniques to overcome the restraining forces in life.
- **RISE to Success** system is a simple, but powerful daily ritual that can help to overcome restraining forces and take us safely to our goals and dreams.

"Positive thoughts have a profound effect on our results in life, but only when in harmony with our subconscious programming."
— Patrice Lynn

---

9 Five Goal Setting Mistakes That Will Frustrate You

Have you set some goals before? Lose 10 pounds, go on a European cruise, increase profit in your business to 30%, start an E-commerce business to earn extra income? Be happier, spend more time with family, start an exercise routine to lower your blood pressure? To use the **RISE to Success** system to your highest advantage, you will want to identify your goals and desires. Knowing how to set a goal is vital. I want you to know right off the bat that most traditional goal setting *does not work*. This is another well-kept secret — it is the "dirty little secret" of the self-help industry.

The leaders in the self-help industry talk among themselves about this. They know most people have not gotten results from what they teach. Amazing, huh? Also a bit shocking. Times are changing, fortunately, and now with brain and heart science, we are aware of what was left out in the traditionally touted pathways to success.

In the last two chapters, you discovered several strategies to overcome your unique restraining forces and catapult to your vision. We identified that beliefs and paradigms affect our subconscious and determine the outcomes in our lives far more than we ever knew. When you apply the simple **RISE to Success** formula, you will override subconscious programming and generate positive results more quickly and with less effort. By adding that knowledge to the ideal way to set goals, you will be unstoppable.

My Personal Experience Goal Setting

In the early days of my career in personal and professional develop-ment, I read numerous books, listened to audiotapes, and took classes on goal setting. I did set some long-term goals and had mediocre success achieving them. I created simple "want lists" of material items I desired that were quite doable. When reviewing those lists later, I discovered that I had acquired most of the items.

As I looked at the goals list from my twenties, which included travel to the Swiss Alps, an income of $200,000+ per year, and a home featured in *House Beautiful* magazine, I felt badly — because I had not achieved those goals. And the worst part was I did not know *why*. Has the same thing happened to you? Maybe you even gave up on traditional goal setting out of frustration and lack of results? In case you have been won-dering why your goals did not work just as mine didn't, you are in luck.

SMART Goals Do Not Deliver — Let's Find Out Why

You can reach your goals without the struggle to make it happen in the often-touted "SMART" goal setting process. Let's unpack this and dis-cover why. First, let's review the meaning of each part of the acronym:

    S – Specific: Define your goal specifically
    M – Measurable: Quantify the goal
    A – Actionable: Action steps to achieve the goal
    R – Realistic: Determine if goal is realistic
    T – Time-related: Set goal timelines and deadlines

We have been conditioned to believe that SMART goals, hard work, step-by-step plans, and willpower are the keys to success. And that SMART goals will get us the wealth and riches and fulfilling life we want. In reality, it can ruin our health and cause frustration and dis-couragement. This has been the recipe of success for decades, but very few became wildly successful this way.

Various gurus convinced us this would work through the often-touted 1953 Harvard Goal Study, which was later found to be false! This study was quoted in every book on goal setting and time management in the

1990's. Tony Robbins, Zig Ziglar, and Brian Tracy spoke about it. The story sounded substantial. Supposedly there was a 20-year analysis of the graduating class of Harvard or Yale. 3% set goals and 97% did not. Twenty years later, the 3% had more wealth than the entire rest of the graduating class. What a great reason this became to set goals. Too bad it was a made-up story.

What do we do now? In the next chapter, you will learn a three-step alternative goal process — the "Sweet Spot". This simple goal system will bring new life and vigor to your ability to reach your goals. For now, let's briefly look at what doesn't work as a foundation for understanding and clarity about what does.

Five Goal Setting Mistakes

1. Outer focused, not inner focused
2. Over emphasis on time
3. Trying to figure out the "how"
4. Over use of willpower to "make it happen"
5. Belief is not taken into account

Imagine yourself in this story that encompasses many of the reasons traditional goal setting doesn't work. Pay attention to what does work. Afterwards, we will look at this piece-by-piece.

Man Turns Life Around With Focus on Inner Qualities

A perfect example of non-traditional goal setting success happened with a switch in focus to the inner qualities versus the outer. A construction business owner was solely focused on the outer results of making a $1 million profit in his business, buying a red sports car, and building a bigger house on a prominent hill. He alienated employees and clients because he was cheep, dishonest, and difficult to work for. The result? He had a terrible reputation.

This businessman met with psychologist and naturopath Dr. Alex Loyd, creator of *The Healing Codes* I mentioned in the last chapter.

Loyd helped him to heal a tough *physical issue* using *The Healing Codes*. Therefore, this man was open to at least listen to Alex's unconventional ideas about how he could achieve success.

Alex Loyd guided him to see the inner world of love, joy and peace as the quickest path to true riches in life. He gave this man very specific instructions and got his agreement to follow them. Over 18 months went by and Alex did not hear a word from this construction owner.

Finally, the phone rang and the businessman relayed his experience. He said he didn't earn $1 million in profit; *he had earned $1.5 million instead.* His reputation totally turned around, his employees loved working for him, and his home life was the best it had been in years. He didn't want the sports car anymore or the house on the hill. He was happy inside.

This man spent more time working on the conditions of his heart and mind, and less time on his business strategies. He and his employees both worked fewer hours and took more vacations, but somehow his business prospered. Dr. Alex Loyd said he was thrilled to hear this news.

1. Outer Focused, Not Inner Focused

The construction owner wanted to be very successful and earn $1 million in profit in his business. He thought he wanted to use that money to buy a specific sports car (for example red Mercedes S class convertible). He thought he wanted a house on the hill (for example specific neighborhood, certain size, with pool, etc.).

In reality, he felt great about improving his relationships with his wife, kids, employees, and the community. This became more important than the material items he imagined he wanted. And from this deeper, happier, more loving emotional place, he created what he really wanted — a life he loved. Because he began treating people with more love, they became more engaged and produced more, and consequently his profit in his business went through the roof.

2. Over Emphasis on Time

When you put a time limit on a goal you may experience stress to achieve it by that time. Many goals are set with strict timelines, which is often counter productive. You can ruin your health, have accidents and increase your blood pressure with an over-focus on time. The tendency to force things might exist with an over emphasis on time. Often, there is a "divine timing" that is out of our control. Going with that flow can be extremely beneficial to help us arrive at our ideal destination.

3. Trying to Figure Out The "How"

Typically, we are taught to create a detailed action plan to achieve our goal. There is nothing wrong with this — you can do it if you want to and if you feel it will help. For example, this may be important when developing a business plan. Yet there are many successful businesses that don't have a business plan.

Many successful people didn't know *how* they were going to achieve their goal until they achieved it.

Outside the realm of what you currently know is defined as "off your radar screen". Don't put your entire focus on what is currently on your personal radar screen because this can be a recipe for failure. On your personal radar screen is everything you see and understand logically. Items might include the money in your bank account, the people you know, the places you go, and your awareness of certain opportunities.

TIP
What Is Off Your Radar Screen Brings the Magic Into Life

The following diagram illustrates a typical radar screen in the middle. Surrounding this radar screen to a distance unknown (possibly to the edge of the universe) are many things beyond your awareness. In reality there are unlimited resources, people, and opportunities outside your personal radar screen, waiting to intersect with you. The "Sweet Spot" defined in Chapter 10 explains exactly how this works.

RADAR SCREEN

4. Over Use of Willpower to "Make it Happen"

An over focus on willpower has gotten very few results for very few people. Often, exerting willpower can cause stress. Who needs more stress? We all have enough, right? Especially as we go along in life, it becomes important to work smarter and not harder. Power is very different from force. As we draw on internal power sources of all types and use less of our own willpower to make things happen, life flows a lot better.

If you want to *Work Hard, Earn Less*:
Use hard work and willpower only to make it happen.

If you want to *Work Less, Earn More*:
Use the power of your imagination and inner world plus inspired action.

5. Belief is Not Taken Into Account

Traditional goals do not emphasize your own personal belief in whether you will or won't achieve your goal as a factor in its achievement. Based on what you learned in the previous two chapters on beliefs and the subconscious, wouldn't you agree beliefs are quite powerful in the equation?

I am here to tell you that awareness of your belief level is important to get what you desire. One of my goals with this book and my teaching, group coaching programs, and retreats is to help you with this. If you don't fully believe your goal is possible, it likely won't happen.

You send out a mental transmission of intention when you set a goal. If you don't believe it will happen, the power of the intention will not be strong. Your lack of belief will send out a counter-intention, neutralizing the wish. This will stop the **RISE to Success** technique from working. Again, "Sweet Spot" goals will reveal what you need to know in the next chapter.

To give you a taste of this new way to get results, following is a **RISE to Success** story:

How I Found My Ideal Car Without Traditional Goal Setting

The last Toyota Rav4 I had purchased was a great car, but not the color I really wanted. When I had my color analysis done in Beverly Hills, Jennifer Butler suggested everyone would benefit from the color of our cars, home décor, and even luggage to be in alignment with our individual color pallet. She said this alignment would bring more joy into our lives.

I found this to be true when decorating my home, choosing clothes, purchasing jewelry, etc. When I bought a Lexus RX350 in gold, I loved that car, and it brought me great joy to drive. However, during the economic crash of 2008–2010, I chose to sell that car. I decided I wanted to buy a more modest and dependable Rav4, and I decided it had to be gold. I chose the year and price I would pay.

Here's the first thing to note: I did not make a plan for *how* I would obtain this car. However, I absolutely believed it was possible to have it, even though Rav4's were in very high demand where I used to live. To set and achieve goals, you don't need to know *how* you are going to do it.

Using the **RISE to Success** process, I immediately located a photo of the Toyota Rav4 I wanted in Google images. I printed out the image and began to visualize myself driving the car and feeling all happy and joyful about the regal gold color and how it matched all my outfits and my personality. Each day I wrote down this passionate desire in my **RISE to Success Journal** and repetitiously imprinted it into my brain.

I spoke out loud and declared what I wanted when I told my friend James about my ideal car. Not once, but two times during the next couple of weeks, he asked if I had looked at the Honda dealer just down the road to see if they had this in-demand item. Well, no, the car I wanted was a Toyota, so why would I want to look at the Honda dealer? Using my logical mind, I dismissed his idea and stayed focused on my desire to buy this car.

One day it just hit me. James is a very intuitive person. The vibration and frequency of this exact vehicle had been sent out by my intention. Sometimes the way things come to us is through other people. Maybe the car was not where I was "planning" to find it, and I should listen to James . . .

With my new open mind, I drove down the road with anticipation. Should you be surprised? There was my ideal car, in my ideal color, from the ideal year, and with the ideal price — *at the Honda dealer*. Wow.

What if I had not listened to my intuition — to listen to James' intuition — and had totally missed it? Instead, within a few short weeks, I was the proud owner of the car *exactly* like the one in my photo. Boy, did that feel good. With a big smile on my face, I drove the car home. Success!

WHAT YOU LEARNED IN CHAPTER 9:
Five Goal Setting Mistakes That Will Frustrate You

To set and achieve goals, you don't need to know *how* you are going to do it. You can release the traditional goal setting process and try something new. Try letting go of these classic goal-setting techniques that could be a frustration to you:

1. Outer focused, not inner focused
2. Over emphasis on time
3. Trying to figure out the "how"
4. Over use of willpower to "make-it-happen"
5. Belief level is not taken into account

When your attitude is right, the facts don't count. Your attitude is 90 percent of the results, whereas the plan, and the *how* is only 10 percent. You will eventually attain all of the people, plans, resources, opportunities and events you need to realize your goal. They will come through the laws of focus, concentration, attraction and creation. Your beliefs, your heart and your positive attitude are the little things that truly make a big difference.

Let's explore that more in the next chapter on a new way to set goals.

Three Powerful Ingredients to Align Goals to Your "Sweet Spot"

10

What are the goals and dreams that are just right for you? *Not anyone else but you*. Not your brother, Richard Branson, Beyoncé, or your best friend. *You*. What experiences and possessions and qualities would make you love your life even more? What do you want to be, do and have in your lifetime? Whatever your unique desire, when your goal is in your "Sweet Spot" it has a greater chance of coming to fruition. Here are the ingredients:

The Inside-Out Approach Works Best to Set Goals

Sweet Spot #1 – Desire that excites me (PASSION)
Sweet Spot #2 – Believe I can have it (POSSIBLE)
Sweet Spot #3 – Good feeling about it (POSITIVE)

In other words, to have anything you want, you must be excited about it, believe you can have it, and when you think about it, feel very good. When any of these elements are missing, you do not have a Sweet Spot. Reaching the goal will be harder. How many times have you identified a goal, but deep down (maybe way, way down in your subconscious) you did not really believe it was possible? You had that nagging doubt — so subtle it was barely noticeable. You didn't really want to pay attention to it because if you did, you feared you might jinx the whole situation. Well, guess what, you were right.

Let's take a look at each of these requirements independently and identify how to make sure you will reach your goals from your Sweet Spot.

Sweet Spot #1 – Focus on What You Want with Intensity and Passion

What makes you come alive when you connect with it? Whatever it is, then do that. In this world, we need more people who come alive and are passionate and on fire for life! Anything is possible when you put your mind to it. Our heart and mind can work miracles in our lives.

There are countless stories of people lifting cars off their trapped children and people who survive climbing disasters by sheer grit. We've talked previously about athletes who win medals by seeing the win over and over in their mind first, wanting it so badly they "could taste it." These are all examples of the power of our heart and minds to focus on what we truly *want*. When you are ignited with passion and intensity for what you want, your mind will go into overdrive to make it happen.

When you give focused attention to whatever you want, it becomes activated. When you lose focus, it becomes dormant. When you add passion to your thoughts, they become powerful to create tangible results. Whatever you love in life will love you back.

Sweet Spot #2 – Believe It Is Definitely Possible to Have What You Desire

Those who believe they can move mountains, do. Those who believe they can't, do not. Belief triggers the power to do whatever it is you want to do. When you act as if it is impossible to fail, it will be. Oprah

Winfrey believed she could be more than a housekeeper. I believed I could move to the *Wild, Wild West* while still in college. Walt Disney believed he could secretly buy land in Florida to build a much larger theme park.

To be successful at aligning goals to your Sweet Spot, first focus on items that have a high belief in your mind. Choose something that you believe is attainable. Don't shoot for the moon if you only believe you can get to Alabama.

Sweet Spot #3 – Your Goal Feels Good and Generates Positive Vibrations

When you know your heart's desire and believe it is possible, the next measure is to feel good when you think about what you want. Do you find yourself smiling and glowing inside? Do you feel joy and satisfaction as you see it happening? Do you feel "large and in charge" or do you feel small, insignificant, or worried? Are you hoping and praying it will really come true? Do you think about contingency plans if it does not actually happen? Confidence, peace, and positive anticipation generate good vibes.

If you feel bad when you think about your goal, it is for one of two reasons:

- You are thinking about what you don't want to happen.
- You doubt you can get what you really want.

Thinking about lack, some people think or say, "I am going to run out of money before I can launch this business." This kind of focus on what you *don't want* will feel bad. You express doubt about reaching your goal when you say, "I just can't do this! It's too hard to lose 50 pounds." Doubt, discouragement, and frustration will feel bad, too.

Once you shift this energy and move yourself to the feel-good happy place, you are on your way. When you feel it in your heart and travel forward in faith, you will land in the Sweet Spot and achieve success. We cover more on this in Part 4: "From Science to the Supernatural". Goals sometimes fail if they are too calculated. This is counter-intuitive to traditional goal setting.

> "Whatever the mind of man can conceive and believe,
> it can achieve." — Napoleon Hill

Let me share with you a fun story about how I set a goal in my Sweet Spot before I even knew it existed. Remember: I have lived my life from a place of trial and error. You get to reap the benefit of all I have learned over 20-plus years practicing personal growth. You can follow along as I tell the story and identify the three ingredients I used that will help you to reach any goal:

Sweet Spot #1 – Decide what you want and be PASSIONATE about it.
Sweet Spot #2 – Believe you can have it and know it is POSSIBLE to achieve.
Sweet Spot #3 – Feel good when you think about it and enjoy POSITIVE Vibes.

How I Was Inspired to Set an Outrageous Goal — In My Sweet Spot

The story begins with a ten-hour solo road trip from Bozeman, Montana, to Denver, Colorado. My destination was certification training for *DISC,* a personality profile. With a lifelong preference for road trips over airplane trips, I decided to drive through the magnificent *Rocky Mountains* as well as the desolate plains of Wyoming to reach my destination. There is very little traffic on this drive and lots of delicious time to ponder and think. *Oh, the joys of a heavenly road trip.*

Typically, I listen to teaching tapes on long drives, and this was no exception. I was enthralled as I listened to a story about a man who set 100 outrageous goals — and proceeded to accomplish all of them! The goals were all quite impressive: have dinner in the White House, golf all the Master's golf courses around the world, and meet famous celebrities. He wanted to be a guest on *The Tonight Show*, meet some world-renowned athletes, learn to fly a hot air balloon, etc. I was flabbergasted. My mouth was hanging open as I drove. I had never even imagined setting so many outrageous goals.

While listening to this story — which I later learned was about Lou Holtz's life — I was so taken by his audacity. In that moment in the middle of desolate rangeland in Wyoming, my mind just clicked, and I made a *decision*. If he could complete 100 outrageous goals, *I ought to be able to do just one*. Immediately and with fervor, I began to dream bigger. He had met so many famous people. I started to wonder, if I could meet just one famous person, who would it be? My mind raced through several popular people of that era. Hmmm, if I could choose anyone, who?

Story: Sweet Spot #1 – Know What You Want, and Be Passionate About It

Out of the infinite field of possibilities, the answer came to me. I knew in my heart the icon I wanted to meet. My sister had given me her workout book, which I read cover to cover and devoured all she shared (to this day, I put my clothes and shoes on standing up because of her). One memorable day in Beverly Hills I sweated my brains out with my sister at this celebrity's *Workout Studio*. This person had a big, positive influence on my life in the area of fitness. She has to this day sold more exercise videos than any one person. "Feel the burn" was her often-quoted maxim of the 1980's. Of course, she is a famous movie star, as well, winning two *Oscars, Golden Globes* and *Emmy's*. I decided she would be a fun person to meet. I made my decision: *I am going to meet Jane Fonda!*

This goal immediately created excitement within me and got my juices flowing. My goal to meet Jane Fonda satisfied the first condition of aligning to the Sweet Spot — *be passionate*. When I returned home, I wrote down my goal on paper: "I want to meet Jane Fonda and spend a half to a whole day skiing or hiking with her." I gave myself seven years (by a significant age) to achieve it.

Within one week, the law of attraction began to kick in and amazing circumstances materialized. Jane Fonda lived 1,000 miles away in Hollywood, the land of movie stars. But all of a sudden the next week she appeared in my town, Bozeman, Montana! I sat back in astonishment. She came to visit billionaire Ted Turner as the two had just started to date. Wow. Within one week of my decision Fonda was within 20 miles of me. Everyone in our small town was abuzz with the news that she was staying at the Gallatin Gateway Inn, and I just happened to be friends with the General Manager.

I called and told him about my goal to meet Jane Fonda, and innocently asked if he could introduce me to her. He said "No", but he shared she was headed to see her brother Peter Fonda in Paradise Valley after her stay at his hotel. Okay, I decided that was something to pursue. Being the resourceful person that I am, I got the idea to call the post office in Livingston and asked for Peter Fonda's address — *and they gave it to me.*

Story: Sweet Spot #2 – Believe It is Definitely Possible to Have What You Desire

Immediately I wrote Jane Fonda a letter and sent it to her in care of her brother. Things were moving *quickly*. Shortly it became even better. I dropped the letter in the mailbox and drove over to my hair salon for a haircut. I had heard a while back from my stylist that the man who had the chair next to her did Peter Fonda's hair. As I sat on the couch waiting for my turn, to my utter amazement Peter Fonda walked in and sat down next to me! Even though the locals all knew Peter Fonda lived close by in Paradise Valley, I personally had never seen him before.

Typical of a celebrity, he wanted to keep to himself and not communicate with just anyone. As he put a magazine over his face, he made that clear. It was just as well. I wanted to respect his privacy, and good thing, because I was *speechless*. At that moment, deep down in my heart, I knew that I would accomplish this goal of meeting Jane Fonda. It would just be a matter of time. Now the second ingredient of Sweet Spot goals was set — *believe it is possible.*

I made another Jane Fonda connection through my good friend who owned a massage business in Big Sky, Montana. This ski resort town is close to Ted Turner's Montana Ranch, and just down the Gallatin Canyon from where I lived in Bozeman. My friend had become Fonda and Turner's new massage therapist. She knew about my goal, but she wasn't about to risk her good client relationship to mention me to them. But she was excited to let me know of her newfound connection to Jane Fonda. And, as fate would have it, through this friend is exactly how I eventually met Fonda a few years later.

Later that same year I experienced major life changes. My husband of five years decided to leave me for another woman he met while traveling as a mountain bike guide. As a result I left Montana and relocated far, far away — across the country in Atlanta, Georgia, of all places.

Almost a year had passed and I had not even thought about my goal to meet Jane Fonda. Then one day a mysterious coincidence happened. After receiving a speeding ticket, I went to court to get it reduced. While waiting on a bench outside I noticed a man reading a newspaper next to me. I glanced over at the paper and spotted a very small headshot of Jane Fonda. I knew about the power of images to visualize a goal, so I made a mental note to retrieve the picture of her after he put the paper down.

Story: Sweet Spot #3 – Your Goal Feels Good and Generates Positive Vibrations

At home I cut the picture out neatly and placed it by my phone. *Everyday* for two weeks I would visualize my goal of spending one half to a whole day skiing or hiking with Jane Fonda. The images were sensually rich in my imagination. I got in touch with how it would feel to have this special time with her in the great outdoors and the feelings — fun, happy, connected, inspired, in love with my life.

After two weeks the phone rang. My close friend said, "I was given two great tickets to see the Atlanta Braves. Do you want to go with me?"

I said, "Yes," and the next thing I knew we were seated at the game, several rows above home plate. I glanced down at the VIP seats and immediately spotted none other than Ted Turner (owner of Atlanta Braves) and his new wife, Jane Fonda. Well, well, there she was. *Talk about fast results*. I visualized for two weeks every day, and she materialized right in front of me in a very unpredictable setting (remember the radar screen?).

Jane Fonda left before the game was over with her girlfriend and walked up the aisle about 10 to 15 feet away from us. Many fans yelled her name and tried to get her attention and, once again, the timing was not right to connect. Our paths had crossed, nonetheless, and the second Sweet Spot — *believe it is possible* was reinforced even more. I felt fantastic and hopeful and excited. I knew this was going to happen and I definitely *felt the positive vibes* — the third Sweet Spot ingredient. From this moment forward, every time I thought about my goal, I felt very good.

My Path Crossed with Jane Fonda's Again Two Years Later

Two years later our paths crossed again. I had moved to Boulder, Colorado and from there traveled to Montana for a speaking gig with *CareerTrack*. I went up to Big Sky Resort to ski and see my friend who owned the massage business. I told her about how I saw Jane Fonda in Atlanta. She still wasn't ready to say anything directly to her about my goal, but she did tell me she was coming in for a massage at a certain time, so I booked one right before hers. After my massage I waited around, but she didn't come.

I decided to leave, and as I was walking down the hall, here came a woman in a very large sheepskin coat with the collar pulled up around her face and a big brimmed hat and dark sunglasses. It was Jane. Remember that star persona I told you about? Short of mugging her in the hallway, this was not the right time to talk with her. However once again our paths had crossed, this time just the two of us, and it felt very exciting. My passion ignited once again and my belief grew stronger. It seemed I was moving closer and closer to my goal.

Finally I Meet My Celebrity Super Star

While on a training tour in Montana, I finally met Jane Fonda. Late the previous night in the hotel an infomercial came on TV. Jane Fonda was promoting an at-home treadmill. I had a premonition in that moment that when I went to Big Sky the next day, we would finally meet.

Seated at a table in the ski lodge at Big Sky with my friend and several of her loyal clients, I glanced around the room. Unexpectedly, I spotted

Ted Turner — and next to him was Jane Fonda. Ah-ha! As fate would have it, when our table was ready to leave, we all stood up, and the famous couple and their party walked right by us. They spotted my girlfriend, their massage therapist, and greeted her with hugs and kisses.

Because of the size of both our parties, it wasn't appropriate for all around introductions. At that time there were very few celebrities bigger than Jane Fonda and Ted Turner. The vibe was to be as low key as possible and not to attract undue attention. Jane did breeze past me, and this time I opened my mouth. "Jane, I saw that infomercial last night with the treadmill — it looks great."

She quipped, "Well, it works," and kept on walking. Okay. I had moved closer to my goal; I got to talk with her. *Yes!*

After everyone in both our parties had moved on, my girlfriend and I stood talking in the lodge dining room in an open area. I was excited about the interaction, but then it got better. I just happened to glance over my shoulder. Who was walking toward us by herself with her water bottle? Jane Fonda, of course. I turned my back to her, faced my girlfriend, and said passionately, "Introduce me!" After all, I had waited patiently for almost five years, and this was *the* moment I had been waiting for.

Jane saw us and stopped, so my girlfriend said, "Jane, I want you to meet my friend Patrice. She has been dying to meet you for years." Here was my moment, and in the beginning I blew it because I said the same thing every other crazed fan has said a thousand times before. "Jane, I am such a fan and really admire your commitment to fitness, and all you have done to help people." I noticed her eyes glaze over with that far away look, and I realized I better say something more personal to get her attention, or the moment would be lost.

Our Goals Overlapped and Created a Win-Win Scenario

Since I had set my outrageous goal I had read that she was now into mountain biking, so I quickly said, "Jane, have you ever been on that mountain bike ride on this ridge right over there?" and I pointed out the window.

She said, "No." But my question triggered her thought of a goal she had made three years earlier to go on a particular hike with her daughter Vanessa Vadim.

Quickly she turned to my friend and asked if she had ever been on the hike from the Spanish Peak trailhead to Lone Mountain Guest Ranch. My friend lied through her teeth (not wanting to disappoint Jane) and said, "Yes."

TIP
You have to be ready when opportunity presents itself

Jane continued, "What are you doing July 6th? Vanessa is coming, and Ted is physically unable to take us on this 18-mile hike. Can you?"

Here I was standing beside Jane Fonda with a goal I set five years ago to go hiking or skiing with her. She just asked one of my closest friends to go on an all-day hike. I had a little talk with myself: "Patrice, here is your opportunity. Speak up — now is the time!"

Time for the Super Bowl Touchdown Celebration Dance

Summoning my courage, I looked at Jane Fonda and casually said, "So, can I go, too?"

She seemed a bit surprised, but thought for a split second, and said, "Sure."

In that moment, I felt as if I had scored a touchdown in the Super Bowl. Inside I was doing the touchdown celebration dance, but outside I was keeping my cool until she walked away. Ha! Truly hard to describe how thrilled and elated I was in that moment. Of course, my girlfriend was very happy for us both, because I was much more of a mountaineer than she was. She wanted me to take leadership of the trip, research it, plan it, and send a letter to Jane Fonda with my recommendations, which I did.

Back in Colorado, two months later, I got a phone call. It was my girlfriend. Jane had gotten back to her. As she said the words, "You got your w — " a loud crack of thunder drowned out the rest.

With eager anticipation, I asked for clarity, "What did you say?"

She responded, *"You got your wish — you are going hiking with Jane Fonda!"* Of course, I was smiling ear-to-ear, jumping for joy and doing that touchdown celebration dance once again. What an exhilarating feeling of *winning*.

The Super Simple Sweet Spot Goal Process

Sweet Spot #1 – Know what you want and be PASSIONATE about it
Sweet Spot #2 – Believe you can have it and know it is POSSIBLE to achieve
Sweet Spot #3 – Feel good when you think about it and enjoy POSITIVE vibes

It's important to note that I did not make a plan to achieve this goal. I did not have it broken down into doable steps. I was not focused on the "how" of the goal. Also, I did not use willpower or over-focus on the time frame. In the center of the Sweet Spot — I knew without a doubt it would happen. And it did, in alignment with the laws of nature.

To The Peak! The Hike of a Lifetime with Jane Fonda

In the height of summer, I drove from Colorado to Big Sky, Montana, and the hike was every bit as magical as I had hoped it would be. Eighteen miles of soaring mountain peaks, babbling creeks, a pristine high mountain lake, and a stormy mountain pass. Ten hours later we reached our destination and had dinner at *Lone Mountain Ranch* after a quick hot tub.

Throughout the day, I had a tight connection with Fonda. At one point, she grabbed my arm and looked intently into my eyes and said, "You seem like someone I have known all my life, but I just can't remember who it is." She added, "If you traced your family tree and I traced mine, I bet we would be related somewhere, because you look just like the Fondas." She made me feel very special. I found us all 4-leaf clovers and she loved that.

Jane Fonda Was Moved to Tears When She Learned About My Goal

Probably the most heartwarming moment happened when we reached the summit of the mountain pass. I told Jane about my goal to meet her and go on a half or whole-day hike. Then I showed the written goal to her. As I told her this was why our day together was so special for me, she started to cry. She called for Vanessa to show her the goal and share the special moment with her. I was truly touched by the humanness of such a renowned celebrity who felt so honored that I would set a goal to meet her. It was a magical moment, for sure.

As we hiked side by side, she said, "Since this is the field you are in, you can speak about this to your clients." She seemed genuinely excited for me. She seemed like a close girlfriend in her affinity and desire for all good things for me. Setting an outrageous goal had turned out to be a very satisfying experience for all of us, and I was filled with gratitude. My ability to set and achieve this outrageous goal also filled me with satisfaction and wonder.

"Aligning goals to your Sweet Spot is the path to turn the invisible into the visible." — Patrice Lynn

---

What You Learned in Chapter 10:
Three Powerful Ingredients to Align Goals to Your "Sweet Spot"

This Sweet Spot goal process works hand in hand with the **RISE to Success** system to create positive results in your life. Once you determine your goal, use **RISE** daily to make it happen. Remember how the daily focus on the picture of Jane Fonda on my desk brought her live into my life in just two weeks? Daily discipline will bring results.

Let's recap this Jane Fonda story in relationship to the **RISE**:

- I thought over and over about spending the day hiking or skiing with Jane — REPETITION. I wrote down the goal on paper and looked at it often.
- Both real pictures and ones on my Image-screen ignited my vision — IMAGES. I played that mini-movie over and over in my mind. I looked at her photo often.
- I spoke the goal out loud and declared to my friends and family I would attain it — SOUND. I believed without a doubt it would happen and said it out loud.
- I felt the emotions; exhilaration and excitement of what it would be like to spend time with Jane Fonda. She had influenced my life in many positive ways and for that I was grateful. Also, I felt gratitude for every interaction along the way that created momentum — EMOTION in action.

Sweet Spot goals provide high excitement, motivation, and good feelings when you think about them. You put the cherry on top when you totally believe you can attain them. Remember the 3 P's: Passion — Possible — Positive Vibes.

PART 3

FROM SCIENCE TO THE SUPERNATURAL

Practical Brain Science & Spirituality — My Journey

11

At this intersection our journey takes a turn beyond the natural world, as we know it, and enters a supernatural dimension. In Part One, the foundation of the four parts to the **RISE to Success** system was built: REPETITION – IMAGES – SOUND – EMOTION. Part Two went deeper into the psyche with insights about change, beliefs, the subconscious mind and how to set goals that really work. Now it is time to explain the science behind the **RISE** through neuroscience, quantum physics, energy, vibration, and frequency.

The world's most wealthy, healthy and happy people have mastered a few simple insights revealed in these following chapters. Ideally, as you read this section your mind will accept the dynamic nature of a supernatural lifestyle as the way you were designed to live. Your life will organically transform with awareness and application of these gems. You will become the person you were meant to be, and as a result the world will become a much better place.

In this chapter there are two segments:

- Segment A — My Journey Into Practical Brain Science
- Segment B — My Journey Into Spiritual Revelation

Come along on my journey as I share how the brain, learning and the basics of the nervous system came to intrigue me. Also, how the supernatural side of my life experience changed the way I see the world forever. The complexity and functionality of the brain does impact our lives and helps to shape results. A spiritual connection with God enriches life in a powerful way. This I know for sure.

Segment A — My Journey Into Practical Brain Science

My brain expertise includes how we learn, overcome obstacles, heal, and create results. With everything I have learned so far I'm quite certain I could have a brain PhD of some sort. However I have taken a non-conventional journey versus a traditional one. Most of what I know has come straight from experts in the field. I attended classes and certification courses led by masters and high-level professionals. I learned "on the job", as I worked as a trainer, accelerated learning designer and ADD/ADHD Life Coach. ADHD stands for "Attention Deficit Hyperactivity Disorder" and is the new umbrella term for Attention Deficit Disorder.

Mentored By Pioneers in Accelerated Learning

My interest in the brain began when I traveled nationally as a *CareerTrack* trainer in the late 1990's and watched people fall asleep in the audience in the afternoon. My contract included daylong lectures and I began to question how there could be a better method than this traditional learning model. Often times in life, results come from asking the right questions. Soon I had the answer I was looking for.

A colleague introduced me to the founders of *Creative Learning International*; pioneers in accelerated learning who lived in my town of Boulder, Colorado. The connection to these brain experts happened when I became certified to teach a course they developed, *The Accounting Game*. Participants in this landmark course learned a whole college semester of accounting *in one day* by going back to childhood to run a lemonade stand. Now that is *accelerated learning*.

We hit it off immediately and joined forces to create a course titled, *The Art & Science of Presentation.* Participants came to understand our amazing brain through the "Left Brain/Right Brain Model" and the

"Triune Brain Theory", which includes three brain regions — reptilian, limbic and neocortex. These brain regions were showcased through fun multi-media skits, colorful props and interactive exercises. We delivered this course and custom programs to Fortune 100 companies across the United States.

The ability to work in harmony with the brain to maximize and accelerate the impact of learning was deeply embedded into my mind and heart through these experiences.

Often I say learning from my mentors was like learning to play the piano from Mozart. I was very fortunate. I learned how the brain works, how to speed up the time it takes to learn, and how to drive the concepts into long-term memory. The power of movement, emotion, and safety in the learning environment has become a touchstone for me. These insights inform all training I design and deliver today, whether online or in person.

Recently in a course on *Micro-learning for Disruptive Results* by Ray Jimenez of *Vignettes Learning International*, the foundational principles of context and content I had learned in the late 1990's were reinforced. Especially vital in today's fast-paced, learn-on-the-go work environments, context is the container, or the perspective that holds the factual content. When a learner understands the context, the content will be absorbed much more easily.

My Introduction to ADHD and Other Learning Differences

In 2001 in Sacramento, California I was introduced to the world of ADHD and other brain chemistry imbalances and learning disabilities. My curiosity launched me into an intense study of neuroscience and I discovered how brain challenges could impact personal lives greatly. I learned that many people struggled with ruined relationships, halted careers, and never-ending emotional frustrations.

Fascinated by brain chemistry, I learned ADHD at its core was a lack of the neurotransmitter dopamine to make the leap across the synaptic gap in the nerve cells of the brain. Due to this deficiency, the chemical loop needed to concentrate and focus effectively was incomplete.

(More illustrations and insights on brain wiring will follow in Chapter 12: "How Neuroscience Programs Your Human Computer").

A lack of dopamine can be supplemented by ADHD medication, like Adderall, which is highly targeted to this part of the brain. I was told these types of medication did not adversely affect the liver and kidneys the way cholesterol lowering medications did. At the time there were a few things that made sense to me. If pharmaceutical drugs existed to help supply dopamine where it was needed, it could be highly beneficial to the person who struggled with ADHD. I also studied research that indicated trauma, toxicity and genetics played a role in brain dysfunction.

Early in 2002 I was able to learn directly from brain researcher, neuro-psychiatrist and bestselling author Dr. Daniel Amen about his unique brain scans. SPECT is an acronym for "Single Photon Emission Computed Topography". Dr. Amen and his technicians looked at blood flow and activity of such areas as the temporal lobe, frontal lobe, limbic brain, and cingulate gyrus through these scan images.

I discovered all of these brain regions have a very practical impact on our lives. For instance, an over-stimulated cingulate gyrus leads to annoying obsessive/compulsive behaviors. A man I knew suffered blows to the temple in a fight with a boy who used brass knuckles in high school. All of a sudden I understood why he had such anger outbursts because his temporal lobe was likely damaged in the fight. The same thing was possibly true about my father who played college football. He developed an unexplained anger problem between high school and college, probably from severe blows to his head.

At *The Amen Clinic* in northern California, Amen taught how brain chemistry, lifestyle and nutrition can make immediate, positive changes in the lives of those with brain disorders. Amen's revolutionary book *Change Your Brain, Change Your Life* was a bright light to many. I learned in person from Dr. Amen who later went on to fame in his PBS specials based on his many books and programs, and today is frequently sought out for his expertise.

My National Tour: *ADHD Coaching as a Proven Component to Successful Treatment*

Dr. Amen gave me permission to use his SPECT images in a course I designed and delivered to medical professionals, schools, drug and alcohol rehab counselors, and fellow coaches who work with ADHD brains. The coaching techniques and brain science I taught during my national ADHD Coaching tour helped participants to better help others with brain and learning challenges.

One excited PhD psychologist gave me excellent feedback. She said my explanation and visual diagram of how the medication she pre-scribed impacts the brain biochemically was the first time she ever truly understood the interaction. She confided to me that she had asked many pharmaceutical reps to describe how the drugs work to no avail. After my workshop she felt more empowered to educate and help her patients as a result.

Managing ADHD in the Classroom was an extensive online course I authored, which was approved in all fifty states for continuing edu-cation credits for teachers in K-12 and colleges. Many teachers were impacted deeply by this training and practical application in their classrooms. Through the course I authored, they finally understood the makeup and challenges of an ADHD brain and how to modify the training environment for higher levels of success.

During this time I also graduated from the *ADD Coach Academy* nine-month coach training program. Here I gained more practical insights into brain function of the hippocampus and parietal lobe, limbic brain, hypothalamus and thalamus. Through the sessions and conferences I attended, I met more experts. As a result, I absorbed more ways to relate to and coach people with ADHD and learning disabilities. I was able to coach ADHD high school teens and adults and empower them to live better lives.

Quantum Physics Bursts Into My Life Through *What the Bleep Do We Know?*

In a quaint theater in Santa Rosa, California in 2005 I watched the debut of the independent film out of Portland, Oregon titled, *What the Bleep Do We Know?* I was mesmerized. The intense, mind-bending insights about quantum physics and neuroscience portrayed on the screen ignited a passion in me and I knew my life would never be the same.

The creative, entertaining way the film taught complicated scientific principles fit right in with my philosophy of how to deliver an accelerated learning experience.

The film was designed as an intriguing combination of three elements:

- Documentary filled with super smart scientists, doctors and researchers.
- A fun story about people and relationships with Marlee Matlin as lead actress.
- Scientific computer animation with phenomenal special effects.

The movie, now affectionately called *What the Bleep,* stimulated my mind to the maximum level. I felt elevated and happy about the whole experience. A couple of noteworthy quotes from the movie are:

- "Quantum physics is the physics of possibilities."
- "Anyone who is not shocked by quantum theory has not understood it."

Currently, I have watched the film at least twenty five times. Repetition is a key to learning, and immersion in this topic has brought more and more insight to apply practically to our lives.

Staying Up-to-date on the Science of Massive Results

In the past ten years I have been studying the brain, neuroscience, chemistry, biology and quantum physics from thought leaders in the field. My mind has been opened and expanded through their books, live workshops, webinars and hundreds of hours of video on *YouTube*. The masters from whom I have learned the most are Dr. Joe Dispenza, Dr. Bruce Lipton, Dr. Alex Loyd, Dr. Caroline Leaf, and John Assaraf and his team of experts and scientists. The results my mentors experience have forever shifted my paradigms about what is possible, and inspired me to take action.

As a result of what I experienced, I saw a need for a shorter, simpler program the average person could easily incorporate into daily life. In our current culture, "how-to" courses are highly popular because our do-it-yourself mindset has grown exponentially. Intuitively I knew there to be a need for my signature program, **RISE to Success**. People want results without having to invest too much time. Fifteen minutes a day is *perfect*.

Practical Brain Science — Highlights of What I Have Learned

- The brain is beautifully complicated in its design.
- Lifelong learning is crucial to keep the brain functioning at a high level.
- An incredible number of options exist to improve brain function.
- The brain responds well to stimulation, variety, fun and setting context.
- Neuroscience explains how thoughts, feelings, images and behaviors originate.
- Quantum physics opens our minds to a world of unending possibilities.

Segment B — My Journey Into Spiritual Revelation

In Part Three of this book, a dance begins between science and spirituality. In the 1980's I heard a prediction that one day in the future scientists and spiritualists would be sitting atop the same mountain. When I heard that statement I was intrigued, but not clear at the time about what it meant. From my perspective three decades later, I see that day has now arrived. Science gives insights into the spiritual, and the spiritual gives insights into science.

There are as many views on spirituality as there are people. As human beings we all seek out the information that confirms our bias, our view of reality, our paradigm. We find what resonates with our bias, and tend to agree with that. During the beta testing phase of this book, I found the people who believe like I do spiritually wanted more of what I was sharing, and the people who don't believe like I do wanted less. That seems only natural.

Quantum physics tells us that the perspective from which we observe life creates our experience of reality. Do you believe in God or do you question, "What is God?"? Are you a follower of Jesus of Nazareth, Buddha, the Dalai Lama, Mary, Muhammad, or Melchizedek? Certainly, I respect your free will to believe spiritually whatever it is you choose.

Personally, it is a risk to step out and share my beliefs and unique life experience with you. My goal in doing so is to lay a foundation for the bridge between science, spirituality and the supernatural explored throughout Part Three. And possibly to connect some dots in a way you may never have thought of before. So, keep an open mind, if you will, and allow my personal spiritual journey to touch your body-mind-spirit in a way that is right for you.

Childhood Influences From Aunt Rosie McKnight, Bob Monroe Original Explorer

My beloved Aunt Rosie led my younger sister and me in our first guided meditation on the floor of our living room in the late 1970's. She was a pioneer in body-mind-spirit exploration, and by my close proximity to her I was highly influenced by her presence. "Relax your toes, relax your feet, relax your ankles", and so it went on up the body.

Anyone remember those types of guided meditations? They were all the same, and at the time that was the popular way to meditate — to physically relax the body so as to enter a deeper, calmer mental state. If I remember, I giggled my way through much of it, missing the whole effect entirely.

My Aunt's formal name was Rosalind McKnight. She graduated from *Union Theological Seminary* in New York City and then moved with her husband, David McKnight, to Virginia. In the *Blue Ridge Mountains* they met Robert Monroe.

The Monroe Institute became world renowned for hemi-sync brain entrainment (used extensively today in meditations), out of body exploration and psychic research in a controlled laboratory setting. By invitation, Aunt Rosie worked closely with Robert Monroe as one of his eight "Original Explorers". She traveled into other parallel dimensions through expanded states of consciousness on a waterbed in a blacked out room. Wired on many levels to the control panel in the laboratory, manned by Robert Monroe himself, her explorations were highly documented.

McKnight wrote two books on her experiences and also taught community college courses in extrasensory perception and parapsychology in Roanoke, Virginia. To this day, in transformational settings, I meet people around the globe who know of my Aunt Rosie and her pioneering work in multi-dimensional travel at *The Monroe Institute*.

Experiencing The Light And Profound Transformation In High School

While growing up in Dayton, Ohio, I attended a very traditional Methodist church. One weekend at a youth retreat there in high school, I met the ultimate inter-dimensional traveler — Jesus. I will never forget the brilliant white light and love like I had never known that flooded the whole sanctuary. Five or six of us, including my sister and two close high school friends, knelt at a wooden rail at the foot of a large, colorful, stain-glass cross. It was here that we asked Jesus to come into our hearts.

At that moment Jesus was connected to me and I to Him for all of eternity. Nothing I could ever do from that day forward would separate me from his everlasting love and caring for me. Nothing. My eyes were filled with tears and the presence of love was indescribable; I was immediately transformed.

Quickly I became a "Jesus Freak". You know, the one with the "Smile if you love Jesus" button and annoying way of turning every conversation to Jesus. No wonder I wasn't so popular at early class reunions.

It's funny to think back on those times and my passionate but ineffective ways.

College Days Bring Many Life Altering Experiences

Probably the biggest shock of my life was leaving my hometown for an Ohio University. For this I was emotionally unprepared. College days brought this kid from a strict home life way too many opportunities to socialize, wander and get in trouble. I was seventeen when I arrived on campus. There was no church youth group, no church leaders, no high school boyfriend or parents to watch over me. Left to my own devices, I threw all caution to the wind and became a thrill seeker, major partier and experimented with mind-altering drugs.

Along with *Apple* founder Steve Jobs and other offbeat visionaries from the 70's and 80's, I eventually came to believe there are merits to mind expanding substances; like the ability to open up new regions of the brain and generate novel ideas. However, the major impact of a party lifestyle for me was damaged health and distorted judgment. The fallout from that was not a pretty picture.

Two stories previously told saved me from continuing down the wrong path.

First of all, my move to the *Wild, Wild West* in Montana put me into a more active lifestyle. Much of the thrill seeking from then on was done on skis, in thermal "hot pots", mountain biking, or climbing rugged peaks — much healthier!

Secondly, when I survived the kidney disease and a near death experience as a senior in high school, I adopted a new outlook regarding wellness. My decision was clear — *no doctor would ever be in charge of my health again.* Granted, it did take me a full two years to get on board completely with this lifestyle plan. After I moved to Montana to finish college, I became a major advocate of alternative health and wellness. As well, living twenty years in Montana placed me in the most pristine environment possible.

Eventually, shortly after graduating from college, I wintered in sunny southern California where it seemed everyone was on the health bandwagon, and for that I will always be grateful. Chiropractic, acupuncture, nutritional supplements, skin brushing, colonics, yoga and aerobic exercise became my new way of life. My body-mind-spirit flourished from that point forward.

Deep Dive Into the New Age Guided My Life For A Couple Decades

In the mid 1980's I lived in the remote backcountry of Montana seasonally while running a secluded but highly popular bar and restaurant, *The Grizzly Bar*. During this time I stayed connected to my Aunt Rosie. She became like a mother to me, as my own mother was more distant at the time. We talked on the phone often and she shared many "New Age" ideas — a term popular at that time to describe new thought and new spirituality. I believe it came as a shortened term from the "Age of Aquarius".

Aunt Rosie sponsored a yearly metaphysical conference through her *Creative Living Institute* in Charlottesville, Virginia, the home of Thomas Jefferson's *Monticello*. The prefix "meta" means "beyond". Metaphysical experiences simply represent anything beyond the physical realm. While there, Aunt Rosie introduced me to angel workers, astrologers, psychics, energy workers, UFO experts and past life regressionists. Quite a ride, I might add, to be exposed to these people and stimulating ideas. Open to everything, I soaked it all in.

During one trip to her conference I had a supernatural experience at Thomas Jefferson's home. I literally felt my cells vibrate at faster rates in certain locations of the home than others. Trees and places on the estate were eerily familiar to me. This had never happened to me before. A couple of times on the public tour I had an internal knowingness about things that happened at *Monticello* before they were revealed to us by the tour guide. A photo of the liberty bell appeared out of nowhere when I placed my arm in my shirtsleeve on my second trip there. The experiences were *beyond bizarre*.

As I processed the strange occurrences (too numerous to share), I somehow left inspired by a new mission to "set the captives free". Jefferson had done that very thing through penning the *Declaration of Independence* — our nation's "mission statement", and also legislation to ban slavery. I remember feeling there was something quite significant about me being there. As if his life and mine were intertwined in some meaningful way that transcended time and space.

On other adventures from 1990–2000, I spent time in the powerful energy vortexes of Sedona, Arizona and learned transcendental meditation in Boulder, Colorado. Outside Mount Rainier, Washington I experienced a channeled entity who taught unique spiritual and scientific concepts at a 3-day *School of Enlightenment* retreat.

The man who exposed me to these unconventional teachings, energetically walk through a wall. His body literally appeared to shift into porous particles that separated enough to go through physical matter. As outlandish as it sounds, I am *not* making this up — I saw it with my own eyes! The crazy thing was, what I saw he later shared was exactly what he intended to do. He was mentally doing the "shape shifting" of his cells as I experienced the phenomena (he was in the advanced class).

Also, at the spiritual retreat was my first ever lesson on neuroscience. We were instructed to draw a brain neuron and the synaptic gap with colored pencils to learn it more effectively — an excellent accelerated learning technique. I still have that drawing. And I still remember the brain science we were asked to absorb.

As you can probably tell, every step on my journey gave me phenomenal experiences and insights. They all shaped who I am today, and fortunately have given me an open mind. Through it all, I never stopped believing in God and I came to value the spiritual dimension, which by then I knew for sure, existed beyond the physical world.

Returning to Higher Energy Bandwidths and a Life of Miracles

While working in southern California during the Dot.com era in 2000, I was invited by a pastor's wife I met at a nail salon to attend a luau at her church, named *Mariners*. You are probably thinking what I was at the time — a luau at a church? It was so out of the norm from what I remember growing up in the super straight, super conservative Methodist church in Ohio. My curiosity led me to go and check it out, and I had fun. As fate would have it, I reconnected with close friends who I summered with in Montana while I was at the party.

As I attended *Mariners Church*, I found it to have upbeat, modern music, the tangible presence of the spirit of God, and a message relevant to my life. Opportunities to meet friendly, wonderful people were abundant. Before long, I felt led to recommit my life to Jesus as the leader of my life. I had wandered around in the wilderness, and just like the shepherd that finds the lost sheep I was enjoying that close, personal connection to God once again.

At this time a *One-Year Bible* was given to me as a gift. The intention of this format is to spend fifteen minutes on 365 daily readings, with the outcome to read the entire bible in a year. Quite a while ago, in high school, I had read the whole bible. When I decided to tackle the challenge again, I never imagined I would keep reading for seven years! The *Word of God* came alive for me and revealed many mysteries of life, some of which included quantum physics principles (see appendix). I found the *Word* to be *alive* and full of life force energy.

When I moved to Oregon, I learned about the supernatural power of the Holy Spirit. The Holy Spirit is another name for the spiritual part of God that exists on earth. This intrigued me, and I attended home groups and witnessed miracles in people's lives. Jesus said whatever He was able to do we would do "greater things". Trained by the best, I learned to do everything *Jesus did* — lay hands on the sick to heal them, receive words of knowledge from God, lead people to Jesus, baptize believers in the Holy Spirit, and cast out demons. You know, just your normal, everyday activities, right?

Previously, I thought all the fun was to be had in the wild goings on in the new age realm, *but I hadn't seen anything yet*. The spiritual truth of the *Word of God* and the phenomenal power of the Holy Spirit reigned above all. I believe this spiritual realm operates above the speed of light and Jesus dwells in the upper bandwidths of energy vibration.

This is how miracles of instant healing are able to happen — through an immediate shift in energy. (More explanation on this in Chapter 13: "Quantum Physics Doesn't Have to Be Hard.")

Supernatural Power to Heal and Transform Lives

The supernatural was alive and well in Oregon and also at *The Healing Rooms* in Spokane, Washington, where I later moved in 2005. Over 3,000 healing centers around the world have been birthed from this one powerful healing place, founded in 1918 by John G. Lake; reopened in 1998 by Cal Pierce.

At *The Healing Rooms* I discovered a world of liberated people, no longer bound by dogma and religion — open, non-judgmental people who facilitated miracles in the name and high vibration of Jesus. I joined the prayer team in 2010 and saw people healed of cancer, blindness, deafness, skin problems, brain damage and physical disabilities of all kinds. People were set free mentally, emotionally, and spiritually. What a gift to join with a group of kind people committed to helping others.

This was a very exciting time of my life including time spent at their *Spiritual Hunger Conferences*. Here I heard for the first time an angelic choir from a higher vibrational dimension blended with the voices of over 2,000 people in the room — quite magical and unmistakable. How else would I have been able to make sense of solid gold dental crowns, gold dust, vapor clouds, and expertly cut, multi-colored gemstones magically appearing out of thin air? This is explained by the mysteries of quantum physics. These are all *signs and wonders* I saw with my own eyes.

More supernatural insights came from a book by Bill Johnson titled *The Supernatural Power of a Transformed Mind* — one of my all time favorites. In his book Johnson enlightens us, "Having a renewed mind is often not an issue of whether or not someone is going to heaven, but of how much of heaven he or she wants in his or her life right now." Do I hear an "Amen"?

As I mentioned, I have always stayed open-minded, don't believe in relying on doctors, and have used whatever methods work to stay healthy, energetic and youthful. From 2010-2015 I worked consistently with an energy healer. She used a unique body scan method to pick up generational patterns, emotional blockages, as well as physical imbalances and energy rifts throughout my body. Through energy healing I found a much greater level of wellbeing. I also adopted green super foods at this time as a high vibration form of live food powders to increase my life force energy and nourish my body-mind-spirit.

Through spiritual leaders I met in Oregon in 2011, I learned about *The Healing Codes* by Dr. Alexander Loyd. Through this God-given, cellular energy healing method, I was quickly healed of an emotionally devastating loss in 2011. In 2013, the codes helped me to discover a rare lifelong trauma pattern, which I was healed from using a variety of methods.

The Healing Codes program works through quantum mechanics and energy directed from the fingertips to power centers around the head. Many others have used this simple six-minute technique to be healed of heart conditions, multiple sclerosis, depression, and cancer. The co-author, Dr. Ben Johnson, used it to heal himself from Lou Gehrig's disease in four months. He was the only medical doctor featured in the popular 2006 movie, *The Secret.* I went through their training and found this Healing Code method phenomenal.

Another doctor I have discovered to be fascinated by mystical experiences and healing is Dr. Joe Dispenza. He was one of the stars of the movie *What the Bleep Do We Know?* Dispenza's newest book *Becoming Supernatural: How Common People Are Doing the Uncommon* documents scientific history made at his workshops around the world. In 2017, I attended his live *Progressive* workshop, which I enjoyed immensely. Common people like you and me have experienced the release of potential, financial breakthrough and spontaneous healing as a result of changes in the brain, heart and connection with God. He promotes his guided meditations as a vehicle to take listeners into the quantum realm beyond space and time.

Today in Sacramento I attend a modern non-denominational church called *Jesus Culture.* I have worked in the children's program called "Game Changers". These 6, 7, 8 and 9 year-old children consistently hear the most precious, beautiful words from God by becoming still within. I have witnessed them receive words of knowledge about other kid's health conditions and lay hands on each other (and adults) for immediate, high bandwidth Jesus healing. They learn there is no such thing as a "Junior Holy Spirit". I am thrilled to be part of a culture where the next generation is raised up to believe they have the *power* within and the miraculous has become commonplace in their lives.

Spirituality — Highlights of What I Have Learned

- Metaphysical means beyond the physical realm of life, typically to the spiritual.
- The universe and everything in it flows from a non-physical reality.
- When we set our minds on spiritual things we can enter the supernatural realm of life. A focus on the material world only, limits our success.
- God in all forms exists in the upper bandwidths of energy vibration.
- There are spiritual dimensions of unending possibilities, miracles, signs and wonders.
- Everything incredible that Jesus did, He said we could do the same and even more.
- The supernatural power of a transformed mind leads to a life of heaven on earth.

Today science and spirituality are eager collaborators in the most exciting time to be alive. Let's continue our exploration to reveal the neuroscience behind **RISE to Success**.

How Neuroscience Programs Your Human Computer 12

Do you have any clue how powerful your brain really is? Imagine the depth and breath of the *entire* Internet with all the interconnectedness and vast storehouse of information. New measurements of the brain's capacity are estimated to be a petabyte, which is 1,000 terabytes — *the same size as the entire World Wide Web.* Astounding. Instead of human and computer, you and your brain are truly the ultimate user interface.

Rest assured, you can program the computer that sits on top of your shoulders to make your life happier, healthier, wealthier and filled with more meaning and purpose. Your life matters and your brain is a gift. Are you ready to receive that gift, open that gift and enjoy its exceptional ability?

Everyday you hold in your hands a cell phone — a mini super computer. The cell phone operates on an integrated system of the following components:

- HARDWARE – iPhone, Samsung, Motorola, LG mobile phones
- OPERATING SYSTEM – iOS, Tizen OS, Google Android OS, etc.
- SOFTWARE – Maps, Calendar, Contacts, Camera, etc.

The super computer metaphor is relevant to illustrate what happens inside of you:

- HARDWARE – Your physical body
- OPERATING SYSTEM – Nervous (brain), hormonal, digestive, energy, reproductive, musculoskeletal, cardiovascular, respiratory and immune
- SOFTWARE – Your paradigms, beliefs, thoughts, cellular memories, feelings

Just like the high tech engineers have a handle on programming our cell phones to do dazzling feats, you can learn to program your operating system and software for optimal results in your life.

RISE to Success is Technology to Program Your Brain for Positive Results

The daily **RISE to Success** system creates small changes in your brain to make you different tomorrow than you are today. Fresh brain connections allow your dreams and goals to become real. As you think, envision, speak and feel in innovative ways results appear to happen magically. However it is a function of brain science and not "woo-woo" nonsensical philosophies. Groups I speak to are quite impressed by this fact. As we watch video clips of the inner workings of the brain, they begin to realize this is based on scientific facts and not fiction. I have found this allows people to accept the premise of this program even more.

The Basic Neuroscience Terms You Need to Know to Activate the RISE

Let's delve into the fundamental science terminology. Ideally some basic brain insights will motivate you to do the program each day, and throughout the day. With each mental intention and activity in the **RISE to Success Journal** you strengthen your internal brain wiring. Theses stronger connections recondition your mind for higher levels of success.

TIP
You can change the circuit wires in your brain by thinking about them

Are you ready for the science? Let's use some accelerated learning techniques:

- We will start with the simplest concepts and build to the more complex ones.

- A few strategically placed metaphors should help you attach the new concepts to something already familiar to you.
- Drawings are designed to illustrate the inner workings of your brain.

My goal is to take you on a journey inside your head where you can see your thoughts as things that impact your physical operating systems listed above.

Neuroscience – The scientific study of the brain and the nervous system.

Neuron – A "nerve cell" is a *neuron*

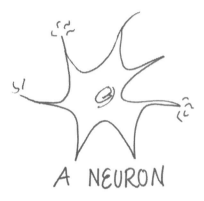

A NEURON

The core components of your brain, spinal cord, and nervous system are neurons. According to biologists, the brain has approximately 90 billion nerve cells. A neuron is an electrically excitable cell that processes and transmits information through electrical and chemical signals via *synapses*.

Synapses – The gap between two nerve cells

Think of a spark plug and the gap in one. A synapse is the connecting point where a neuron passes an electrochemical signal to another neuron. Like a spark plug, the electrical current and chemicals interact in the synaptic gap to rapidly fire off a new impulse or thought. Literally the same way your car moves due to the electric current lighting the gas on fire; your thoughts ignite in your brain synapses between neurons with chemicals that you produce. These chemicals are your *neurotransmitters*.

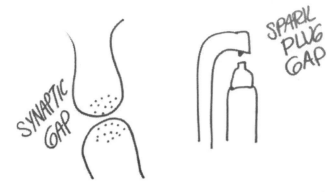

Neurotransmitters – Chemical messengers

Neurotransmitters enable communication between your neurons. Examples are proteins and hormones. Both are crucial for cellular communication in your body. The hypothalamus, in your inner brain, coordinates two systems for sending instructions to your body: your nervous system (electrical) and your endocrine system (chemical).

- Every time you have a thought, you produce a chemical.
- Negative thoughts create chemicals that make you feel bad.
- Positive thoughts create chemicals that make you feel good.

These electro-chemical instructions travel on branches called *dendrites/axons*.

Dendrites/Axons – Nerve cell branches, similar to tree branches

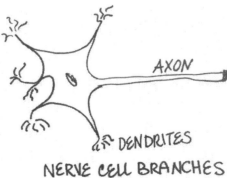

Dendrites and axons are the branches of the neurons that join with other nerve cells to create *neural networks* through electrochemical stimulation. Generally, axons transmit and dendrites receive signals. They are constantly moving and reaching for new connections, which by the way you impact moment by moment by your thoughts. There are trillions of potential connections available.

What happens when you read these words? In a few hundred milliseconds the signal spreads through nerve cell branches (axons) to the synapses (connecting points) to a receptive neuron and then to billions of neurons in several dozen interconnected areas of your brain — and you have a perception of what the words on this page mean. Isn't it incredible how much happens at lightning speeds?

Neural Networks – Clusters or groupings of interconnected neurons

NEURAL NETWORKS   PEOPLE NETWORKS

Imagine reaching your hands out to others in the world that share your beliefs, and joining hands with them. A business network or a social network is like a *neural network*. You meet new friends and colleagues. You disconnect from some people and form new connections with other people — always changing, always evolving. Experts say to pay attention to the people you associate with because you will become like them. Similarly your neural networks are based on frequent associations to what you think, see, say, feel and do.

Associations are formed in these "neural nets" (abbreviation for neural network). All we know in life is attached to a neural net. Ex.

Prosperity - as you experience, feel, identify and know prosperity you create a *neural net* for it in your brain. Our subconscious mind is made up of these ingrained connections. The good news is they can be redirected. You can change these associations at any time because of a beautiful thing called brain *neuroplasticity*.

Neuroplasticity – The brain's ability to continually form new neural connections

Unlike previously thought by brain experts, *our brain can change!* Neurons in the brain will adjust to new thinking, learning, behavior and new environments. This allows you to break free of past pre-wired connections, which is called *synaptic pruning*, and create new more useful ones. The more you think deeply the more branches you grow. The more you think correctly the more healthy networks you build in your brain and the more intelligent you become. Isn't it kind of crazy that we can choose how intelligent we are by directing our thoughts?

Our brain and nervous system have the ability to rewire based on what we focus our attention on in life. You become what you think about most of the time. Huge brain activity happens when you redesign your brain via directed and disciplined ways of thinking. *Our thoughts make a difference*. Activate the **RISE** and see results:

- Catapult your business or career.
- Expand your income.
- Enhance your relationships.
- Attain a new level of happiness.
- Become the person you were meant to be.

Neurogenesis – The brain's ability to generate brand new neurons

Hopefully you are encouraged as I am to know that no matter your age or life circumstance, your brain can and will create new cells. Previously thought to be static, your brain is full of life force energy and transformational power. Dr. Caroline Leaf is a PhD scientist and author of *Who Switched Off Your Brain* and *Switch On Your Brain*. Based on neurogenesis, Dr. Caroline Leaf was able to help a young girl with extensive brain damage regain and surpass her previous IQ. She also rejoined her school class within an eight-month time period and graduated with honors. Not long ago, doctors and scientists declared this to be impossible.

What "impossible" situation in your life needs to hear the good news of the nature of the brain to regenerate, renew and re-energize?

Mirror Neurons – The brain's ability to understand another human (empathy)

TIP
Positive thoughts and words regenerate your brain

Mirror neurons give us the ability to feel what it feels like to do something simply through observation in close proximity to another person. Earlier in *Chapter 7: Demystify Beliefs to Improve Health, Wealth and Happiness,* one of the ways identified to reach "unconscious competence" is to watch a master perform a skill. Mirror neurons enable you to duplicate their actions. Kinesthetic learners feel through their mentor's demonstrated ability of expertise. These feelings duplicate brain neurons.

Mental Rehearsal Grows New Brain Circuits

As you picture an idea of who you want to become, and rehearse it over and over, you will grow new neural circuitry in your brain. Consider these **RISE to Success** actions: The use of REPETITION to mentally rehearse your chosen IMAGE everyday creates a model of who you will be in the future. As a result:

- The brain on a synaptic level will look as if it has had the actual experience you imagined.
- Your body operating systems will begin to physically change without you having the real life physical experience.
- Your internal efforts make it real in your mind, in your consciousness.
- Beautiful long-term relationships are then built in your neural networks. Just like friends you associate with frequently, the neural connections get stronger and stronger the more time you spend together. They become more familiar.

As you learned, neurons fire electrochemically, hence the concept of "brain wiring". Similar to electrical wires that turn on lights at home, your brain can be programmed or "wired" for success or failure. No matter your current reality, you can rewire your thoughts, images, words and emotions toward your ideal vision of the future.

Hardwired Pathways Become Automatic Brain Programs

TIP
Learn every day to create new neural pathways in your brain

Our personal daily habits determine how many new neurons and new neural networks are created. Would you like to generate new networks for "money", "happiness" or "success"? Neural pathways are hard-wired by repetitive patterns. Habits are controlled by the subconscious mind and will become automatic, or unconscious.

Love to learn because it creates a chemical rush biologically in the body as new neural pathways are created. This can be addicting, but quite a positive addiction and one all effective leaders and super successful people share.

When your mental habits are life giving and empowering, you orchestrate a beautiful symphony in your brain. Chaotic thoughts roving through your head are very disrupting on an emotional level, and they damage your brain (hear heavy metal music). As you take control of your thoughts, you will interrupt any habitual negative processes before they produce harmful chemical reactions in your body.

Use Neuroscience To Hardwire A Life You Love

Memories that are emotionally charged release more chemicals and therefore create deeper neural pathways in the brain. Just like a well-worn path in the grass commonly seen when people cut corners on a college campus, or at a park, for instance. Over and over people walk in a certain path, and before long it is a deep dirt groove in the lawn where grass can no longer exist. Your brain also develops grooves that become the "paths of least resistance" as you trod along on them over and over.

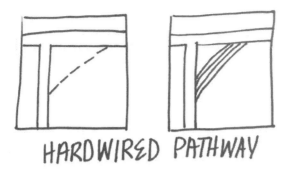

HARDWIRED PATHWAY

Earlier you learned when you think a thought, a brain chemical (neurotransmitter) is released into your body. It can be positive or negative. Did you know you could actually become addicted to emotional chemicals generated within

TIP

We can evolve ourselves by changing hardwired patterns in our brain

your brain? The more you pay attention to your moods, your vibe and habitual ways of responding to life, the more you are able to choose how you respond. When you're able to think greater in your mind than how you feel in the body is when change happens.

RISE to Success is about training you to go beyond your circumstances, moods, and environment to choose the high level emotional state your desire.

Negative Spiral Down

- Every time you have a thought, you make a chemical.
- Negative thoughts create chemicals like cortisol that feel bad.
- When you feel bad it is because you thought a wrong thought.
- How you feel typically impacts your future thoughts.
- This is a *problem* because it determines how you are "being" in any moment.

Positive Spiral UP!

- Every time you have a thought, you make a chemical.
- Positive thoughts create chemicals like serotonin that feel good.

- When you feel good it is because you thought a correct thought.
- How you feel typically impacts your future thoughts.
- This is a *solution* because it creates how you are "being" in any moment.

The **RISE to Success** simple, daily system is designed for common people like you and me to take control of our lives and create empowering brain habits. Each day you take charge of what you think, write in your journal and do the activities; millions of brain cells align, fire and move together in the positive direction you set. Add energy, emotion, intention and the results you seek will come rushing toward you:

- More clients, more money, more friends, and more opportunity.
- More happiness, more peace, more love and more joy.

Kick Fear and Anxiety to the Curb

The added benefit I have discovered of a daily **RISE to Success** habit is to expel fear, anxiety and doubt. Happily these low-level emotions are driven out by my constant focus on the good things I want in my life. The well-worn positive images in my brain replace any former undesirable images, thoughts and feelings. Each day I override the habitual negative emotional states for which my brain cells were previously accustomed. As I write and speak, I change from the inside out. I feel and act differently, and therefore positive results show up in more abundance.

A Few More Helpful Brain Mechanisms to Use to Your Advantage

A. Brain Compass: Reticular Activating System — "RAS"
B. Brain Thermostat or Set Point

A. Brain Compass: The Reticular Activating System — "RAS"

Because most of us drive a car, the best way to illustrate the power of the "RAS" is one we all have experienced. When you drove a silver Acura, you didn't even notice the blue Prius on the road. But as soon as you bought the blue Prius, *you now see a blue Prius everywhere*. The same holds true for the new boyfriend or girlfriend's vehicle — you see their car everywhere the moment you felt the love vibe with them.

My girlfriend Mary Jo recently visited me in Sacramento. She told me she bought a Ford Flex. I told her I wasn't sure what they looked like. She mentioned you don't see them very often on the road. As soon as she left, however, I spotted my 1st Ford Flex in a parking lot. Now I see them almost daily. That is my "RAS" at work. I am now tuned into seeing her car.

The Reticular Activating System is a collection of neurons in your brain stem. The "RAS" acts as a filter to include/exclude into your awareness the people, places, material items, and circumstances you focus on, and deem important. When you decide what you want and imprint it into your subconscious, your "RAS" will guide you toward it like a compass directing a ship to port.

The Reticular Activating System is a powerful brain compass that will take instructions from your conscious mind and relay them to your subconscious mind. When you decide exactly what you want, write down your goals and desires every day, imagine and speak them out loud, your "RAS" helps you to achieve them. The entire **RISE to Success** system is designed to activate your reticular activating system — use it to your advantage!

B. Brain Thermostat or Set Point

Apparently each one of us has a financial and emotional thermostat set at a certain level. It works the same way as your thermostat at home. Once set at 70 degrees (whether sun, wind or snow outside) the heating and cooling systems work to keep the temperature inside at 70 degrees. The thermostat calibrates consistently to maintain that preset level. Money and happiness, for instance, are preset in our lives based on a myriad of factors, until we change the thermostat.

Did you hear about the study done on lottery winners and paraplegics? Incredible as it may seem, after one year both groups had the same happiness level. As you might imagine, initially, the lottery winner was ecstatic and the paraplegic was depressed. These extreme feelings existed only because of what *they expected* would happen due to this magnanimous life change.

Over the course of the year the paraplegics became more empowered and could do much more than they previously imagined. Emotionally, mentally and spiritually things were quite similar to life before the accident. However happy they were before is how happy they ended up.

Sedona Film Festival Movie About Paraplegics

At the Illuminate film festival in Sedona, I watched a documentary *Rebound* about a group of guys in wheelchairs who formed a competitive basketball team. They had each other's backs, gave each other hope, passion and a reason to live. The story was beautiful. At the climax of the film they won a championship tournament and a few players were awarded athletic scholarships to attend college and play basketball. Some of them said getting paralyzed was the best thing that ever happened to them!

Meanwhile, lottery winners thought the financial windfall would make them much happier than it actually did. Remember what I shared earlier — people think if they *had* a million dollars, they could *do* anything they wanted, and then they would *be* happy? In reality, these lottery winners moved forward in life with all the same emotional, mental and spiritual challenges (aka baggage) they had before. Statistics show most lottery winners end up in the same financial position as they were before the deluge of cash, and with the same happiness level.

Same thing can happen with highly paid professional sports players who blow all the big salaries they earn. When they get hurt and are unexpectedly forced to retire, they are potentially worse off than when they started. They may have gotten used to the high-income lifestyle, which has now come to an abrupt halt. They may be just as happy emotionally, however.

Bottom Line: Your brain thermostat controls your emotional and financial set points. Therefore, the emotional aftermath of a wildly fantastic stroke of luck, or a devastating catastrophic calamity will essentially leave you just as happy as you ever were.

"Most people are about as happy as they make up their minds to be." — Abraham Lincoln

Daily **RISE to Success** will enable you to turn up the dial on your thermostat and reset it to a higher and happier level. Make up your mind to become happier and wealthier, and program your brain to these

> **TIP**
> You create a life you love when you use neuroscience to your advantage

new levels. Brain neurons that fire together, wire together. You absolutely have the ability to wire your brain for the specific results you want.

WHAT YOU LEARNED IN CHAPTER 12:
Neuroscience Programs Your Human Computer

In a survival mode we live the same reality over and over again. Our brain thinks a certain way 90 percent of the time and programs the neural environment to create our internal state. We live in a default mode and that is what we get — conditioned behavioral responses that are "no-brainers".

There have been movies made like this. Each day the character wakes up to find the same life scenario facing them. Typically, it happens over and over until they have an awakening, change their paradigm or have a life-altering event. Then a shift happens.

Through our frontal lobe, our conscious brain, we have been given the ability to choose.

- Choose your thoughts and emphasize the positive.
- Choose your words which have the power to create good things.
- Choose your pictures on your Image-screen to bring your dream to life.
- Choose your emotions to lift your mood to a high vibration.

Move Beyond Survival and Use Neuroscience to Achieve Success

In this chapter on neuroscience you learned it *is* possible to change your thought patterns and hardwire happiness and other positive results into your brain. We do have control over our neurons, neurotransmitters, neural nets and neuroplasticity of our brain. As you understand the inner workings of your brain, you will find science is on your side.

Our journey from science to the supernatural gets especially interesting as we open the door to the quantum realm. In the next chapter we will explore the basic tenets of quantum physics and how this "wacky world" will help you to make your dreams come true.

Quantum Physics Doesn't Have to Be Hard — Here's Why 13

When I grew up, a favorite television show in our household was *The Twilight Zone*. Fascinated by science fiction, fantasy, psychological thrillers and unexplainable phenomena, I would wander into these Rod Serling adventures with boundless delight. Maybe these early explorations explain why the magical, mystical world of quantum physics intrigues me.

Quantum physics is a world *unknown* by most people on the planet. Quantum physics is a science of the unseen realm. That is, except for the scientists with high-powered microscopes who discovered and documented its findings. Most people hear little bits and pieces about the subject, and think it is too complicated to understand. What about you?

As your fellow space traveler, I will help you focus on the simplest and most practical aspects of quantum physics. I won't bore you with every last detail and all the research to back it up. I like simplicity, too. Only the quantum basics are needed to understand how the **RISE to Success** daily system delivers positive results into your life. Who knows, maybe by the end of this chapter you will become a fan like me.

"The most beautiful thing we can experience is the mysterious. It is the source of all true art and science." — Einstein

You Live in a World of Physical and Non-Physical Reality

Quantum physics identifies a large part of our universe to be non-physical. Everything you actually see around you is portion of a vast ocean of incredibly small particles. Under certain conditions these particles shift into waves — *waves of possibility*. Right now you may think you hold a solid object in the form of a book or a tablet in your hands. Crazy as it may seem, quantum physics confirms that your physical body *and* these objects are blinking in and out of physical reality.

How can this be true? And how are you an integral part of this twilight zone scenario? Classical physics identified earlier as Newtonian physics (discovered by Isaac Newton), states what you observe as being "out there" is really and truly "out there". On the other hand, quantum physics states that what you observe to be "out there" actually depends on what you *choose to observe*. What you choose to focus upon.

For instance, you are able to see something internally on your Image-screen in your mind that is not yet real in this physical dimension. You have a vision, an idea of what you would like to happen: a career in music, a doctorate, and a popular personal brand. When you see it, by your observation it transforms from a wave of possibility into a particle. At that moment your vision is one step closer to reality — because you just made it real in the quantum field.

TIP
Mind influences the behavior of physical matter

We have all heard it before, "Your thoughts create your reality". Well, new quantum physics studies support this idea. Can you see why it is important to be purposeful about what you see and what you say? *You just might get it all*. We are literally reality producing machines.

However, most people don't affect reality in this way *because they don't think they can*. And that is exactly why I wrote this book. I want you to know the powerful truth to help you intentionally create the life of your dreams. Let's review the **RISE to Success** parts from a quantum physics perspective:

- REPETITION of thoughts are made of energy and affect matter.
- IMAGES are made of energy and affect matter.
- SOUND vibrations are made of energy and affect matter.
- EMOTIONS are made of energy and affect matter.

Quantum Physics Definitions

- "Quanta" means energy.
- "Quantum" are packets of energy.
- "Quantum physics" is the description of the smallest things in our universe. Atoms, molecules, and subatomic particles and how they work and interact with light.
- "Quantum mechanics" and "quantum physics" are essentially the same thing.
- "Quantum fields" are forces described as fields that mediate interactions between separate objects. Similar to electronic and magnetic fields with localized vibrations, these fields span all of space.
- "Unified field" is another name for the quantum field, coined by Einstein. These fields are mathematical theories of quantum physics.
- Everything that exists is a consequence of giant energy fields vibrating.

"The entire universe is made of fields playing a vast, subatomic symphony." — Don Lincoln, Physicist

Matter is Not Physical and Solid Like We Thought

As mentioned earlier, throughout time we have been led to believe that matter is physical and solid. Actually it is 99.99999999% empty space! Matter has the illusion of being solid because as we are experiencing these items they have slowed down in vibration to a solid state. Gases vibrate the fastest, then liquids, then solid matter.

Remember back to science class when we learned about atoms as the basic building blocks of matter? There was a nucleus, a little dot in the middle made up of protons and neutrons. We also learned there were electrons circulating in a cloud around the nucleus with positive and negative electrical charges that did something to keep it all functioning. I'm stretching here to remember, can you?

ATOM

Quarks are the Smallest Known Units of Matter

With the advent of new technology and stronger and stronger microscopes, we are now able to look deeper into the atom and find out the nucleus is not the dense dot we all learned that it is. The protons and neutrons of the nucleus are made up of hadrons, which are made up of quarks. Super tiny "Quarks" are currently the smallest known fundamental units of matter. All of these elements are called "subatomic particles".

To help you make sense of the "wacky world" of quantum physics, it may be helpful to know where the term "Quarks" came from. Theoretical physicist and professor Murray Gell-Mann is credited with creating the meme of quarks. Gell-Mann chose the name "Quark" from a reference in literature, "Three quarks for Muster Mark!" in James Joyce's comic fiction book *Finnegan's Wake*. Comforting, right?

What Materials Make Up Our Cars and Our Bodies?

Turns out, everything on our planet is made of the same material — *atoms*. Even rocks on Mars are made of atoms. The combination and the ratios of the atoms are what make each substance unique and make them appear different in the physical world. The numbers of potential combinations are virtually infinite.

To give you the big picture, let's dive into some objects you are quite familiar with: your car and your body. Put your science hat on as we analyze these substances.

What type of material is your car made of?

- Metal, steel, plastic, leather, cloth, computers

What are those substances made up of?

- Molecules

What are molecules made of?

- Atoms

What are atoms made of?

- Subatomic particles

What are subatomic particles made of?

- Energy!

What type of material is your body made of?

- Digestive, endocrine, muscular, nervous, reproductive, respiratory, skeletal, cardiovascular and elimination systems

What are those systems made up of?

- Tissues and organs

What are tissues and organs made of?

- Cells

What are cells made of?

- Molecules

What are molecules made of?

- Atoms

What are atoms made of?

- Subatomic particles

What are subatomic particles made of?

- Energy!

"Everything we call real is made of things that cannot be regarded as real." — Niels Bohr, Quantum Physicist, Scientist

---

Everything is Energy – Vibration – Frequency

Quantum physicists like Einstein, Planck, Bohr, and others discovered that physical atoms are made up of vortices of energy that are constantly spinning and *vibrating.* Each atom is unique because the distribution of its negative and positive charges, coupled with its spin rate, generates *a specific vibration or frequency pattern.*

The physical laws of nature state everything has a vibration. Albert Einstein said that everything in life *is vibration.* Sound is a vibration and so are thoughts. The chair you sit in, the coffee you drink, the shoes you wear, the house you live in, the river you kayak — all are made up of vibrating packets of energy, not solid dense matter. This is the subatomic world. These particles all vibrate at different energy frequencies. Everything you see and touch is nothing but unique vibrations.

Simple Science Terms Defined

ENERGY: Energy is proportional to frequency ($E \propto f$). Everything that exists is made of energy. In physics, energy can be transferred to an object and can be converted in form, but energy cannot be created or destroyed. The higher the frequency, the more energy an atom has. And everything in the universe is made of atoms.

VIBRATION: Oscillation motion of a fluid, solid, light or electromagnetic wave, which radiates through the vacuum of space. The expanding ripples in a pond from thrown pebbles illustrate vibration. Sound is simply a mechanical vibration that passes through a medium such as gas, liquid or solid to become a sound. Everything that exists has a vibration.

FREQUENCY: Mechanical vibrations; audio sound signals, radio waves and light waves. Frequency is the rate at which something occurs or is repeated over a period of time. A radio station broadcast or transmits signals through a waveband at a certain frequency measured in hertz. The normal brain frequency in the awakened state is 14-100 HZ.

BANDWIDTH: A range within a band of wavelengths, frequencies, or energies. Describes the volume of information per unit of time any medium, like an Internet connection or radio, can handle without distortion. Popular culture also describes bandwidth as the mental capacity or energy a person has to deal with a situation.

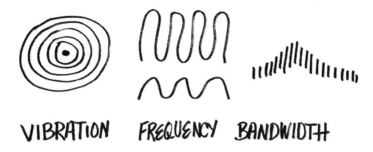

VIBRATION   FREQUENCY   BANDWIDTH

Practical Applications of Energy and Quantum Theory

Let's continue this discussion with items and topics with which you are already familiar. Because energy fields travel easily through the physical body there are many scientific instruments that use energy to work. The entire computing infrastructure is due to quantum physics. Here is a list of medical devices and other energy based items:

1. Lasers – acronym for Light Amplification by Stimulated Emission of Radiation
2. Semiconductors – silicon chips in every computer and cell phone in the world
3. Microprocessor – electronic component on a single integrated computer chip
4. MRI - magnetic resonance imaging medical device
5. Electron microscope – uses beam of accelerated electrons as source of illumination
6. CAT scans – acronym for Computerized Axial Tomography medical scan
7. PET scans – acronym for Positron Emission Tomography medical scan
8. Nuclear/Atomic power plants – use nuclear fission and fusion to generate power

Hopefully, these examples take some of the mystique out of quantum physics and energy. It is highly likely that *every day* you are being impacted by these discoveries. And until now, you may not have been aware of this fact. Consequently, it shouldn't be a stretch to realize you can use quantum physics to achieve your goals, program your brain, shift your energy, illuminate your imagination, and amp up your words.

Three Basic Quantum Physics Principles

Next, our journey will take us a bit deeper into the complexity of quantum physics with three of the most basic principles on which the science is based. We will also begin to shift into the supernatural world through some of the following explanations and examples.

1. Quantum Superposition – The Power of Focus
2. Quantum Entanglement – The Power of Relationships
3. Quantum Zeno Effect – The Power of Mind Over Matter

1 - Quantum Superposition — The Power of Focus

Particle And Wave Duality

The famous physicist Albert Einstein came up with the idea that sub-atomic particles (electrons, protons, neutrons, etc.) are both waves and particles at the same time.

- Particle: Light (photon) is a particle – static
- Wave: Flow of photons is a wave – fluid

PARTICLE   WAVE

Quantum "superposition" means matter can exist in more than one place at a time — until we choose and all collapses into the one. Matter changes from particles to waves based on the behavior of the observer. When you are "looking" it is a particle, when you aren't "looking", it becomes a wave of probability. As the observer you are in a sense authorizing what you see.

TIP
Your view of reality affects particle and wave duality

In Quantum superposition, two things can exist at the same time. How can this be? Imagine if you will the following scenario:

- Your body is standing still.
- Your body spins in one direction.
- Your body spins in the other direction.
- Now you spin in both directions at the same time!

The scenario seems entirely impossible until you consider how a magnetic resonance imaging (MRI) works. Have you ever had an MRI scan? Twice from accidents, once for my knee and once for my shoulder, I had MRIs. I lay still while that big machine spun around me capturing images. Unlike an x-ray or a photo, magnetic resonance imaging enables us to see inside ourselves through *the superposition of hydrogen atoms*. An MRI literally makes them spin around in both directions at the same time. Strange, yet true.

What is spinning in two directions at once in your life? What will you choose?

Practical Application: You are the Observer and Creator of Your Life Experience

You are truly the observer and creator of your life. As you have by now learned, there are infinite "waves" of possible choices we can make in life. They are all happening at the same time. With free will and clarity of vision we can choose, and collapse the wave into an actual reality, a particle. When you are crystal clear about what you want - your choices and intentions literally impact physical matter. Your thoughts become things.

Hold those ideas in your mind as you read this story about the founder of the women's clothing line *Spanx*, Sara Blakely. Sara had a sea of possible choices she could make, until one day, every potential coalesced into one clear choice.

Sara Blakely Asks for and Receives a Sign to Pursue Her *Spanx* Idea

Sara Blakely invented *Spanx* — the immensely popular undergarments and clothing that flatter a woman's figure. In 2000, *Spanx* fashion apparel took the industry by storm, being named to *Oprah's Favorite Things*. But what is the backstory to how this good fortune came her way?

Much earlier in her life, Blakely's experience as a salesperson in Florida required her to wear pantyhose in very hot and humid weather. Immense discomfort sparked the initial idea to cut off the feet of her pantyhose. She wanted the control-top under her slacks without the unattractive look of the hose when she wore open-toe sandals.

Blakely played with the idea that other women just might feel the same way. She looked for a manufacturer and took all the necessary steps to patent and produce the under garments. But suddenly, she questioned her efforts. Would other women support her idea? Would anyone by them? Should she invest the little money she had left? In that moment of doubt, she paused and asked for a *sign* to reveal to her whether this was truly the right path.

Blakely returned home that day and did what every woman of the 90's who needed a "time out" would do. She plopped down on the couch and turned on *The Oprah Winfrey Show*. To her utter amazement, there was Winfrey talking to a guest about cutting off the feet of her pantyhose to avoid the look of hose in her sandals. Blakely couldn't believe her eyes as she watched the image of Oprah flipping up the bottom of her dress to show the audience her cut-off pantyhose.

There was her sign!

Sara Blakely immediately knew she would invest her last $5,000, and pursue the manufacturing to develop her idea. If Oprah needed it, she knew other women would also buy her products. Her vision was clear and she took massive action.

Today Blakely is a self-made billionaire, and her company *Spanx* is a household word.

All the possibilities for the future of Sara Blakely's life existed in quantum superposition. When she fixated on her one clear choice, she turned a wave of potential energy into a particle of reality. Her powers of observation and clear vision determined her next steps. Blakely catapulted into mega-success with the power of intense focus to collapse the energy of her ideas into physical matter.

2 - Quantum Entanglement — The Power of Relationships

At a subatomic level all particles are connected, related, *entangled*. The quantum realm is so much bigger than we can imagine; there is no time, no space, no distance. Imagine all the cells in your body, trillions of them, all connected to each other. Now move out of your body as you lie on a blanket gazing at the stars, trillions of them, all connected to each other by the universes in which they exist. When you see a star it is not always a real object; it is the memory of that object projected in light years to your eyes.

Everything is connected and with quantum entanglement you have free access to everything that exists. We are all one — I impact you — you impact me. Quantum entanglement happens when you think of someone and then the phone rings and there you are — magically connected with them on the phone line. Have you ever been talking to someone and all of a sudden you know what he or she is going to say next?

Quantum entanglement also explains why cellular memories from trauma are still present in our body-mind-spirit today as if they just occurred. These memories from past events with people are entangled in our energy fields. They exist at a cellular level until they are released through the power of God to heal them through prayer, energy healing or transformational methods.

Practical Application: "Spooky Action at a Distance"

Experiments have been done with a group of people who come together and pray to decrease crime in a certain area. Statistics before and after the experiment show crime was indeed decreased. The sound and thought vibrations of the prayers reached the higher dimensions and impacted physical matter at a quantum level. These energy signatures travel through space as invisible waves similar to ripples on a pond. "Spooky action at a distance" is a term Einstein coined to describe how matter can be impacted without touching it, even at far distances.

United States Government Human Cell Experiments

An excellent story that reveals the power of quantum entanglement is found in a 1998 experiment at the United States Department of Defense. They scraped cells from a person's mouth and placed them in a test tube. They moved the test tube to different rooms, then different buildings and eventually to a distance fifty miles apart. The person whose cells they used was hooked up to a lie detector or polygraph, as were the cells in the test tube.

They played soft, soothing music and showed calming television shows to the person. The researchers then switched to chaotic music and violent shows. In every case, whatever response was happening to the person, the cells in the test tube registered the exact same activity even fifty miles away — hence the "spooky action at a distance" effect of quantum entanglement.

Also, there are movies and real life stories of people who have received a heart transplant or a liver transplant from a person who was dying. The living recipient magically takes on many of the qualities of the person who donated the organ to them. The cells of both people, deceased and living become entangled. The distraught loved ones who miss their family member are now energetically connected to them through this new person. Heartwarming, these stories powerfully illustrate this quantum physics phenomena.

Quantum Entanglement Comes to Light in My Jane Fonda Story

Peter Fonda lived close by me in Paradise Valley, Montana for 15 years, *yet I had never seen him anywhere before*. Moments after I sent a letter to Jane Fonda via his address, and dropped it into the mailbox, I was seated next to him on a couch in a hair salon. The best explanation is that our energy fields were entangled on a quantum level. And there we were together at the same exact time and space.

Jane Fonda had set a goal to take her daughter on *The Spanish Creek Trailhead Hike* for three years. I had set a goal to meet Jane Fonda and go hiking or skiing with her for five years. As I look back I realize the vibrational frequency I sent out to meet Jane Fonda was an exact match to her vibrational frequency. Boom! No planning, no phone calls, just pure aligned energy. "Spooky action at a distance" explains how I was in Wyoming and she was in California when I set the goal to meet her, and the next week we were supernaturally twenty miles apart in Bozeman, Montana. We had a relationship connection before we met through our shared vision.

Verrrry interesting . . .

What if the genie in a bottle from the fairy tale that will grant our wishes is actually *you* and *I*? Our wishes might seem to be luck, coincidence, or serendipity. Yet when we put out a specific frequency at the strength to bring the particular wish into our physical universe — *the experience will find us*. This is true manifestation.

In the discussion on goals we discovered the resources you need to reach them are often off your radar screen outside your conscious awareness. The area off your radar screen is where the people, opportunities, events and circumstances currently exist. That is why you don't have to be concerned about "how" to make your goal happen. Life is a cooperative journey among powerful individuals. We are all connected — we are all entangled. Things can appear "out of nowhere" and find you! All you have to do is be clear about what you want and use **RISE to Success** daily to imprint it powerfully and repetitively into your energy field.

3 - Quantum Zeno Effect — The Power of Mind Over Matter

The quantum zeno effect defines a cause and effect between mental and physical phenomena. This is the point where neuroscience and quantum physics overlap. Moving from science to the supernatural includes:

- You become what you focus on.
- Energy goes where your attention flows.
- Your mind does affects physical matter.

"Quantum physics supports the notion of mind over matter."
— Dr. Caroline Leaf, PhD Scientist, Author of *Who Switched Off Your Brain*, and *Switch On Your Brain*

If we believe it, it is true. If you think you can or think you can't, you are right.

What we think and believe impacts, changes, and moves physical matter. The fully conscious, aware mind trumps both nature (genes) and nurture (environment). You can program yourself to experience a joy-filled life. Focus is directed attention and is a function of the mind. The energy and intensity of your thoughts directly influence your health and wealth and ultimately, your quality of life.

> **TIP**
> With every thought we are creating our life

Practical Application: Attention and Vibration Impact Physical Matter

My personal friend, Bob Shontz, has the most relevant story of "mind over matter" I have ever heard. Let me warn you — this is truly hard to believe, *but is absolutely true*. Besides hearing a firsthand account, I viewed the proof through hospital photos and surveillance video of this event.

Man Recovers from Gunshots Using Mind Over Matter

While driving away from a meeting in Las Vegas, Bob Shontz stopped at a traffic light. He had an intuitive warning about a man who was walking towards him from the right, but he ignored it. Next thing he knew the man jumped onto his truck running rails, and started shooting him — *several times!* A bullet lodged in Shontz's head and his shoulder.

His very first thought was "I'm alive, alert and I feel great!" His next thought was to pull into a casino across the street to make sure the shooter was apprehended. That was his only objective. He ran into the lobby to tell them about the man. Obviously, blood was gushing everywhere, and the staff on duty communicated the obvious to

continued

him, and decided to call an ambulance. He reiterated, "I feel great." He didn't even want to get on the gurney, but the first responders made him lie down in order to be transported to the hospital.

When he got there, doctors removed the bullet out of his skull while he was totally coherent. "I didn't take any medicine, no drugs, anything", Shontz relayed. "It is all in your thoughts. The mind is powerful." His brain started to swell, he had bleeding on his brain and they wanted to put him into intensive care for three days, but he refused. They were not able to remove the bullet in his shoulder.

Even though the doctors argued with him to stay, he decided he really wanted to go home. He said, "I'm fine. I am coherent. I am going home." He signed the papers to be released from the hospital. They let him go. Shontz went home, laid down in his recliner and did his "due diligence" (Obviously part of the magic sauce, but Shontz did not reveal exactly what this entailed). Six hours later he woke up and all the swelling was gone.

When asked how he did it, he said, "You are either at effect, or you are at a cause over your life. I was in control", Shontz said. He also shared that he had been through mind training. He learned there how to control his vibration, his thoughts, and his energy and even to change his DNA.

Three days after the shooting Shontz spoke on stage in front of an audience. He had no side effects, no swelling. On the fourth day, just before he flew to Zurich, Switzerland, the doctors wanted to check him over. He went in for an x-ray to check on the second bullet that had lodged in his shoulder. *It was gone.*

Bob Shontz made the grueling eleven-hour flight four days after he was shot in the head and shoulder — as if nothing had ever happened! Eventually, there was not even a scar where the bullet had entered his head.

Shontz's final comments regarding his phenomenal recovery from the shooting, "It is all about vibration. That's it."

Bob Shontz's story is remarkable. And so is this next story. This final story may have bits of all the quantum physics properties that have been highlighted: quantum superposition, quantum entanglement, and quantum zeno effect.

Supernatural experiences exist in the metaphysical aspect of life; beyond the physical world. This one in particular demonstrates the power of spiritual beliefs infused into high vibration sound waves. Truly a fascinating account of the influence of the spoken word mixed with positive expectation is recounted in this true story about a packaging company:

Commanding Particles to Realign for Business Success

Gunnar Olson owned *Alfapac*, a family-owned business in Europe that made packaging materials out of high tech plastic film. One year they had readied 1,000 pallets of large plastic bags for agriculture use for shipment the following week. Made over a five-month period this one shipment, worth several millions of dollars, comprised the bulk of their revenue for the entire year. Unfortunately, during a routine inspection they discovered all the plastic bags had mysteriously been laminated shut. They were ruined. Several engineering and manufacturing experts were consulted with no clear resolution.

The owners came together as a family to talk about solutions. In his mind, Olson heard the words "If you have faith like a mustard seed [which starts out very tiny and grows immensely tall], you can speak to your mountain and heave your mountain into the ocean, and it should obey you." He resolved to speak these words to the bags.

The family owners held hands, surrounded the pallets, and Olson shouted at the top of his lungs, "Listen heaven and listen earth! Who is in charge of *Alfapac*? Jesus is in charge! In His name I command all those plastic molecules to migrate back!" They laid their hands on each pallet, which took three full hours, and then they went home in peace.

continued

Upon returning to the plant early Monday morning, they saw all the employees opening the packages that contained the bags. *Not one plastic bag was sealed shut.* A miracle had happened and the company was saved from financial ruin. (Story recounted from You Tube video titled "Gunnar Olson Plastic Bag Testimony")

Apparently, the power of Olson's spoken words and his deep faith had resonated in the quantum field where anything is possible. Remember, everything in the material world, like the plastic bags, is made up of atoms. All atoms are made up of vibrating packets of energy, not solid dense matter. Doesn't it make sense now that *energy-vibration-frequency*, the raw materials of life, can be changed by our thoughts, words, images, and emotions?

Descriptions of God include: omnipresent (exists everywhere at once), omnipotent (all powerful), and omniscient (all knowing, including the past and the future). Remember, "quantum" means energy and these are quantum concepts. God created the heavens and the earth, and created us in His image. Therefore, we are empowered to be co-creators of our lives. What if many people live below their potential because they really do not grasp the unlimited nature of our quantum reality?

WHAT YOU LEARNED IN CHAPTER 13:
Quantum Physics Doesn't Have to be Hard — Here's Why

The capacity you have to reach into the supernatural realm and bring treasures forward into your life is astounding. You can call those things that are not as though they are — from energy into matter. The quantum field, vaster than the galaxies, will respond. Remember this every day. Never be limited by what you see and feel. There is so much more available to you. The universe is truly unlimited, abundant, plentiful and friendly.

1 - Quantum Superposition – The Power of Focus: Quantum superposition means matter can exist in more than one place at a time — until we choose and all collapses into the one. Matter changes from particles to waves based on the focus and actions of the observer.

2 - Quantum Entanglement – The Power of Relationships: Everything is connected and with quantum entanglement you have free access to everything that exists. We are all one and linked in mysterious ways. "Spooky action at a distance" is a term Einstein coined to describe how matter can be impacted without touching it, even at far distances.

3 - Quantum Zeno Effect – The Power of Mind Over Matter: What we think and believe impacts, changes, and moves physical matter. The fully conscious, aware mind trumps both nature (genes) and nurture (environment). You can program yourself to overcome physical and mental challenges and experience a joy-filled life.

From science to the supernatural — all of these dimensions empower the **RISE to Success** system to work in your life. Success is not just financial or material; it also encompasses a mind-body-spirit approach to life.

14 The Brain Secret of The World's Most Wealthy

The world's wealthiest people control the greatest number of resources on our planet. Today Oxfam reported that the 8 richest men in the world possess the same amount of wealth as the poorest 3.6 billion people combined. According to Forbes, the number of billionaires has grown over the past 30 years from 49 in 1987 to 1,826 in 2017.

Previously, monopolies owned by the rich included salt, railroads, banking, oil and food. New monopolies include technology, ecommerce, computers, clothing and media.

Have you ever realized what you purchase is controlled by a small number of elite business people who play monopoly in real life?

What are the secrets of this select group of people? What do they know, and do, that we don't? If you aspire to have more wealth maybe you have sought knowledge in an effort to become more enlightened on the subject. Perusing popular thought on "secrets of the wealthy" leads to tips such as:

- Use other people's money
- Understand value over cost
- Use of time
- Play to your strengths

- Have a big vision
- Take risks

Maybe a case could also be built for "luck" being a major ingredient in success. After all, *Facebook* founder Mark Zuckerberg was a college student at Harvard when he was approached to build the platform for someone else. Was he simply "in the right place at the right time"? Also the tried and true "whom you know" or "who knows you" could certainly be true for career politicians who end up as mega millionaires.

Granted, hard work, good decisions, vision, and stellar money management are not to be put down as avenues for wealth creation. What I am going to share just happens to be in a totally different category. Consider this revelation as beyond the logical path, beyond the world system, but as something you can easily combine with traditional methods. The only way you will know how well it works is to apply it in your life and see what happens.

The secret is one I learned from a man worth hundreds of millions, and likely something you have not heard previously. I certainly hadn't. As a matter of fact, the moment I learned this insight is when I knew I had to bring **RISE to Success** to all of you. The brain secret of the world's wealthiest was totally aligned with the processes I had developed gradually over many years. Yet, I had only begun to tap into its unlimited potential myself. And as I did, significant things began to happen. What I discovered is this: incredible science applied to our lives is a stealth vehicle to take us further into the supernatural realm and a life we dream about.

Before I reveal the news, let's review a few principles relayed in this book:

- **Brain Science:** Your thoughts and feelings are electro-chemical reactions in the synapses of your brain neurons. Chemicals from positive thoughts and emotions feel good, and from the negative feel bad. Through the power of your conscious mind you can choose positive thoughts and feelings over negative ones.

- **Quantum Physics:** Everything that exists is made of atoms and subatomic particles — which are all made of energy. All forms of energy vibrate at unique frequencies. Energetically you are connected to a field of unlimited possibilities. In this quantum field are unlimited resources outside your current awareness. Your body-mind-spirit affects physical matter in all forms around you.
- **Positive Ball of Energy:** Daily repetition of positive thoughts, words and deeds programs your subconscious to generate an abundance of good vibrations. Clearing out negative cellular memories and limiting beliefs cancels negative vibes and frees up energy. When the positive ball of energy you emanate becomes bigger than the negative ball of energy, a major shift occurs and everything in your life gets better.

The #1 Brain Secret The Super Wealthy Do Not Want You To Know:

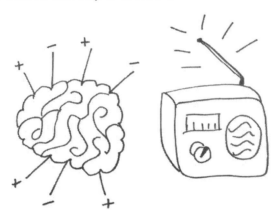

Our Brain Is A Transmitter And Receiver Of Energy Frequency

- Our brain broadcasts just like a radio station.
- Our brain also has a volume/power control and tuning dial.
- We have the ability to create any frequency we want and transmit it at any time with any speed and velocity.
- Brain radio-like frequencies are picked up/received by similar frequencies throughout the world and impact physical matter around us.

- Our brain has the fastest electromagnetic frequency of any transmitter on the planet — faster than satellite, radio and cell tower transmitters.
- Our brain sends out broadcasts of energy that travel in all directions at once and transmit instantaneously with no loss of power — 2 feet away or across the world.
- Brain transmissions pass through any matter like an invisible gas that can go anywhere — through elevator doors and walls.
- Frequencies we send out affect physical matter and bypass space and time.

In case you wonder about the validity of these statements, keep in mind scientific geniuses Albert Einstein and Thomas Edison said the exact same thing decades ago. They agreed the human brain does transfer, and also receive, measurable energy frequencies and vibrations.

Once you know these brain facts, you can use this secret to your advantage. Along with the other insights in this book, you are able to take control over your life and results. At any time day or night you can visualize radio antennae extending out from your brain. Send out specific thoughts, images, words and emotions and you will attract people and abundance into your life. Send and receive specific energy vibrations into the field of infinite potential and God will meet you there. Ask and you shall receive.

Everything is energy and that's all there is to it. Raise your energy for more life force and more power. People and things will be drawn to you. When you match the frequency of the reality you want, you cannot help but get that reality. As you send out more good vibes you will draw to yourself like vibrations. This is not philosophy. This is science and physics combined to create a supernatural experience and a life you truly love.

Consciously Send Out Positive Energy Vibrations From Your Brain

First get clear about what you want: be it a new job, different car, weekend in Lake Tahoe, positive performance review, or special birthday present for your daughter.

The speed the "wish" will come into your physical experience depends on:

1. **Intensity:** Increase the power of your transmission — grab ahold of it with your focus and your emotion and imagine you already have it.
2. **Frequency:** As often as possible for as long as possible — ideally when you feel good and are upbeat is when you transmit the energetic frequency of what you want.
3. **Consistency:** On a constant basis, day after day, is the most effective.

You now have a daily **RISE to Success** ritual to focus and direct your brain broadcasts.

New Activities You Can Do With Just Your Thoughts

Let's put a little traction onto these statements with some new experiments being done to show the power of our minds to affect matter. These experiments involve the use of our brain to do the following with our thoughts (our transmissions):

1. Dial a phone number.
2. Open an email.
3. Move a cursor on a computer screen.
4. Play a computer game.
5. Control a robot's arm.
6. Change the TV channel.
7. Adjust the volume of the TV.
8. Control a character in a virtual reality movie.

Essentially, we may soon be able to be operate like Alexa or Siri to operate items around our house with our minds; call or text friends, do simple house cleaning, find radio stations, play music and turn on a certain movie just by thinking about them. These advances prove how powerful our brain really is and the potential we have to focus our energy.

TIP
Where you place your attention is where you place your energy

Thoughts represent units of energy. Invest in thoughts that are productive and manifest the reality you want. Be energetically frugal. Everything you do in life you put out energy. *Thoughts consume energy.* Make sure they are uplifting and positive and you will surely create optimal results.

We cause our atoms to spin and vibrate at a particular rate by what we think, believe, see, say and feel over and over. A new layer of awareness is built on our daily system:

REPETITION + IMAGES + SOUND + EMOTION leads to our SUCCESS!

Pay Special Attention to Your Thoughts and Feeling Vibrations

Our thoughts are all made of different vibrations. If a thought is positive and makes you feel good, it vibrates at a higher frequency. Ex. "I love you." If a thought is negative and makes you feel bad, it vibrates at a lower frequency. Ex. "I hate you." The Emoto experiment with sounds and words taped to glasses of water demonstrated the impact of subtle energy frequencies on water molecules.

Remember to pay attention to your feelings. How you feel is an indication of your vibration. Your vibration sets up the attraction. When your emotions are positive, your vibration is high - you will attract positive results into your life. The world around you is responding to who you feel you are in your body and who you believe you are in your mind.

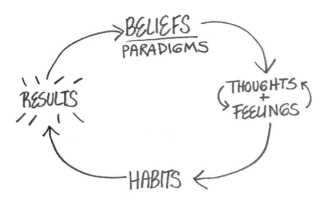

Science now reveals matter is actually impacted by our thoughts and beliefs. What makes up "things" are not things, but ideas, concepts and information. Here are some practical ways to express this. Have you ever:

- Communicated to your car and noticed it performs better?
- Called your car a pile of junk and find it always breaks down?
- Talked to your plants and observed they are green and healthy?
- Got mad at your body for frequent colds and are rarely able to get well?

"The day science begins to study non-physical phenomena, it will make more progress in one decade than in all the previous centuries of its existence. To understand the true nature of the universe, think in terms of energy, frequency and vibration."
— Nikola Tesla, Inventor and Physicist

How I Used RISE to Success to Meet My Mentor — Just as I Imagined

June 1st, 2017 was a very special day. I was privileged to meet my quantum physics mentor and superhero, Dr. Joe Dispenza. He is a pioneer in the field of neuroscience, quantum physics and personal transformation. I have been following him over the years since he starred in the aforementioned movie, *What the Bleep Do We Know?* He has taught me so many incredible things and I enjoy his meditations immensely. For who he is, and the impact he has had on my life, I am forever grateful.

Using the techniques I write about here, I was able to get a last minute front row seat to Dr. Joe's small, intimate *sold out* event in Sedona, Arizona at the *Illuminate Film Festival*. Every day for 3-4 days leading up to the event, I activated the IMAGES portion of my **RISE to Success** system in my **RISE to Success Journal** in the following way:

I wrote a paragraph of what I wanted to happen and turned it into a movie production on my Image-screen. Next I focused intently on it for 2 minutes at a time in a sensually rich fashion. I felt and expected what it would be like to attend his lecture, speak with Dr. Joe one-on-one, get an answer to a question from him and get my picture taken with him . . . all of which happened within a few days! *And,* I might add, he was very unavailable to the public, for questions and photos. Earlier at the *sold out* 100-person seminar I noticed he bolted out of the room with no interaction with people at all.

Likely he had to protect himself energetically, because so many people want to get close to him. Dr. Joe Dispenza had become extremely popular because his message resonates with so many people, and over 100,000 have attended his workshops in person. He relayed that attendees have experienced incredible results with his meditations and teachings.

At the smaller *sold out* seminar I grabbed a seat *in the front row* on one of four chairs placed perpendicular to the audience, along the wall. These chairs were not released for anyone to sit on — until I arrived! The room was packed to the brim and these special seats remained untouched, almost as if they were invisible. I had visualized the front row and that's exactly what I got. I walked into the packed room and I asked if there were any seats up front, and the response was, "Yes there are. Right this way . . ." Dr. Joe stood so close to me I could have reached out and touched him.

Afterwards, the premier of the movie HEAL was shown at the *Sedona Performing Arts Center* auditorium which was filled with over 1,000 health-conscious people. Dr. Joe starred in the movie HEAL and shared many stories of his participant's success accessing the quantum field and moving in space and time beyond "self". During the panel discussion after the film premier, I was one of two people with the honor to be handed a microphone and able to ask Dr. Joe a direct question (something else I envisioned during my **RISE to Success** visualizations).

continued

After the panel ended, I acted courageously to connect with Dispenza from the stage. I waved to him and asked if we could have our photo taken together and he said, "Just a second" as he finished up with the producers of the movie. Moments later he walked closer to me and said, "So, you want me to come over to the edge of the stage, and kneel down so you can get a photo of us together?" I confidently replied, "Yes!" How could he say "no" to such an enthusiastic, adoring student as me?

You gotta love moments like this.

It was obvious to me that through the visualizations I did, we had already met in the quantum realm. My brain was sending out the perfect vibration and frequency to attract him into my energy field.

Dr. Joe Dispenza and I talked and I told him how I have followed him from the *What the Bleep* movie to now and have learned so much, but never attended a live program. He enthusiastically suggested I attend one of his live workshops, where he promised to "Rock My World!!" He teaches all over the world, and I had missed his workshop the previous weekend in San Diego. I made the decision to stay put in Sedona to continue writing my **RISE to Success** book and be present for the film festival.

As fate would have it, just after meeting Joe, I ran into the lovely energy worker Leah Denmark Starlight, in the aisle of the *Sedona Performing Arts Center*. She was the one who told me Dr. Joe and Gregg Braden have taken their work to a whole new level, and that she occasionally speaks on stage with them. A few days earlier when I knew Dr. Joe would be in town, I had asked if she could introduce us, but she said he would be unavailable for such meetings. I was smiling from ear to ear as I showed her the pic I just had taken with Dr. Joe. (Remember the "neural networks" we can build in our brain cells, which are similar to networking in person?)

I mentioned to Leah that Dr. Joe suggested I attend one of his live events. I expressed how much I would love to go, and she excitedly said, "There is one in Las Vegas next weekend!" Wow - I did not know this information. Just a five-hour drive from Sedona, Las Vegas was on my way to my next stop in California. Hallelujah! What a blessing Leah had been in my life — you could say all of this happened because I met her, in line at *Staples* in Sedona of all places! (Another example of quantum entanglement and the power of relationships)

Once again reinforcing the power of **RISE to Success,** I envisioned this magical moment with my mentor, Dr. Joe Dispenza exactly as it happened in reality. Meeting Dr. Joe was an enlightened experience I will never forget. What a lovely and memorable day — filled with high vibrations, beautiful connections and gratitude.

I created this mental movie of my desired interactions with Dr. Joe in my mind first. When I did the **RISE to Success** practice over a span of just a few days and it came true, I realized I literally created the experience out of the airwaves. I accessed the quantum realm where there is no space and time and everything is possible. I broadcast the perfect energy frequency and made my vision come into reality.

As I contemplated this experience days later, I came to a conclusion. I felt quite certain that no one else in the room of 1,000 had this level of *focus and clarity* and took the time to *create* it mentally and emotionally first. I am sure there were others who would have liked to have the experience I had, yet, they didn't put the forces at work ahead of time to make it happen. My efforts through a very simple 15-minute daily **RISE to Success** process made the waves of possibility collapse into particles of reality. *Ta-Da!*

What if the intensity, frequency and consistency in which I rehearsed this moment brought it into reality? What if my brain sent and received the exact energy vibrations and frequencies to attract Dr. Joe easily into my energy field and life experience? What if you could create the same experiences on demand, any time you want? What if using **RISE to Success** is the answer you have been looking for? You will never know how you can use your brain as a radio transmitter and tune into the prosperity, happiness and fun moments you desire until you get started and find out for yourself.

Law Of Attraction Works Even if You Are Unaware Of It

Now with a deeper understanding of energy, vibration and frequency the "Law of Attraction" can be presented effectively. Simply put, what you transmit is attracted to you. Attraction is the most senior law and defies all laws. More senior to "Law of Lift", which is more senior to "Law of Gravity" and why planes and birds can fly.

The "Law of Attraction" exists and can be used successfully whether you are focusing on it or not. Even if you use it unconsciously, instinctively, and through trial and error it still works. Anyone can be unaware of the strength of the law, but still use it to their advantage because it is a natural law and works all the time. That explains why some very wealthy people may have never heard of the #1 Brain Secret, but when asked, they are actually using it. The success of the process is most effective when you know the mechanics and apply them in the right ways.

Reminder of the #1 Brain Secret:

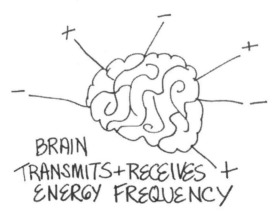

BRAIN TRANSMITS + RECEIVES + ENERGY FREQUENCY

Our Brain Is A Transmitter And Receiver Of Energy Frequency

Why Don't World's Wealthiest Want You to Know This Brain Secret?

Many wealthy people, dating back to Henry Ford, did not want to empower the general population with this brain secret. Preferably the masses were to be kept on assembly lines of their factories, dutifully earning minimum wage — followers, not leaders.

Andrew Carnegie, in a break from tradition, hired Napoleon Hill to research the wealthiest people at the turn of the 20th century. Hill was commissioned to write about the principles of success and to share them with the public in a book. Napoleon Hill spent decades on the project personally interviewing titans of industry and the wealthiest of the era. The result was the classic book titled, *Think and Grow Rich*. But, legend has it; some things were forced out of the book — including the brain transmission idea I shared with you in this chapter.

Not everyone has our best interest in mind, right? There are people in this world whose only aim is for power, influence and control over others. Fortunately for you and I, more and more people exist who want everyone to succeed. They are willing and able to impart a wealth of knowledge on abundance and wellness. Fortunately, I have been learning from these people, and now am able to share these insights with you.

TIP
Brain Science Holds Valuable Keys To Our Success

Whether or not you believe the basis of what I am sharing with you, the fact remains; there is only one way you will truly know if it works — *try it out for yourself.*

Mindset Habits of the Brain's Most Wealthy:

Here are a few mindset habits of very successful people. You will notice, the goal in each situation is to keep your vibe at a high level and keep feeling good:

- Spin bad news to be positive. "I'm not sure how this will work out, but it will." You must believe it when you state it. *Feel good* right now regardless of what is going on.
- No matter what happens, say, "This is the greatest thing that's ever happened!" and add to that the belief, "It will all work out just fine."

- Sometimes what appears to be *bad* usually turns out to be a blessing. And it could even mean that something *good* is about to happen. Instead of getting upset, acknowledge it as something good. Do not let yourself feel bad about the event.
- When you get a taste of bitterness about something or someone, you can use the event to clearly define what you don't want — and then turn it to a positive and clarify what you do want.
- Learn to *dial in* the exact brain frequencies that you want to better transmit the highest-level frequency and attract excellent opportunities.

How to Build More Positive Vibrations and Increase Your Positive Ball of Energy

There are a few daily habits all high performers share:

1. Read books every day (readers are leaders).
2. Listen to CDs/podcasts/audio downloads/YouTube each day.
3. Attend live events with like-minded people — collective brains synchronize.
4. Build relationships that edify and acknowledge others accomplishments.
5. Associate with people that have what you want.
6. Have a morning ritual to start your day on a positive note.

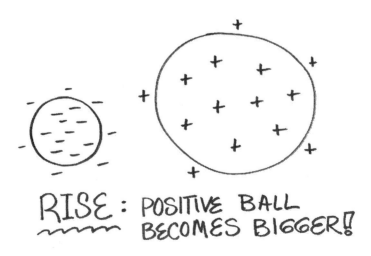

RISE: POSITIVE BALL BECOMES BIGGER!

WHAT YOU LEARNED IN CHAPTER 14:
The Brain Secret of the World's Most Wealthy

- The #1 Brain Secret of the World's Most Wealthy is that your brain is a sender and receiver of energy vibration and frequency.
- Direct your life by your vision, not your logical mind. The real secret is to focus every day on feeling good now and raising your energy vibration.
- 99% of things that will make your wishes come true are *off* your radar screen, beyond what your naked eye sees.
- Focused brain transmissions will pull in the people, opportunities and events you want and need from the quantum field of potential.
- Business it is not about putting all your effort into marketing strategies, hard work and finances. High vibration thoughts and feelings trump all else.
- Early in the morning, throughout the workday and at night preparing for the following day, train yourself to feel good about the things you desire.
- Elevate your thoughts with gratitude, love, joy expectation and excitement.

As you practice and perfect this process, your life will become much more to your liking. You will experience more flow, fun, and all the benefits of a rich, fulfilling life.

PART 4

THE BEST TOOL TO REWIRE YOUR BRAIN

Best Tool to Rewire Your Brain: RISE to Success Journal 15

> "What you think, imagine, say and feel creates your personal reality." — Patrice Lynn

Throughout the previous sections of this book you have come to understand the 4 basic segments of the **RISE to Success** simple daily system: REPETITION — IMAGES — SOUND — EMOTION. You have also learned the role our inner psyche plays in creating our results. You also know that science and spirituality are pathways to the magic of the supernatural world. Now you will learn very practical *how-to tips* to use everyday in the **RISE to Success Journal**.

#1 Secret to a Successful Start to Each Day

In a nutshell, the number one secret to sustainable success is to be present, positive and mindful each day with *a powerful morning routine*. Many famous top achievers like Warren Buffet, Tom Brady, Richard Branson, and Oprah have very focused and purposeful morning routines. They claim this *positive start* impacts the rest of their day and their incredible results. And some of my mentors: Dr.

TIP

Own the first hour of the day and you own the day

Joe Dispenza, Jim Kwik, Dr. Alex Loyd, Dr. Caroline Leaf, John Assaraf, and Jim Bilyeu also invest time in their own unique morning rituals.

You can do this, too. This is why I created the **RISE to Success Journal**. I researched this topic and found some common characteristics of morning routines of successful people:

1. Water
2. Exercise
3. Meditation/visualization
4. Inspirational reading
5. Mindfulness breathing
6. Gratitude journaling
7. Write down goals/intentions
8. Declarations/affirmations
9. Time with loved ones/pets
10. Healthy food

Here are key things many high achievers say NOT to do first thing in the morning:

1. Look at cell phone (especially while still in bed)
2. Check email
3. Listen to negative news
4. Get distracted from priorities

It is no coincidence that five of the ten common characteristics of successful people are contained in the **RISE to Success Journal**. They are meditation/visualization, mindfulness breathing, gratitude, goals/ intentions, and declarations/affirmations. Obviously you can combine your journal routine with other items from the list, and even some of your own favorites. I personally drink a full glass of water first thing every morning, brush my teeth with my left hand, exercise 5-10 minutes and eat a healthy breakfast – along with my daily **RISE** morning routine. Hopefully these insights will reinforce further the benefits of this tool to rewire your brain for success, and give you a positive fresh start everyday.

Before I share how to prepare yourself for the daily **RISE** activation ritual, let's begin this section with a success story of how I used the principles I am teaching you to bring about an incredible business opportunity.

How I Manifested an $8k/Month Income

At a point in my life when I wanted to create more income through new assignments and new contracts, I turned to the **RISE to Success** formula to create an $8,000/month income. To start, I made a creative page full of images in my **RISE to Success** workbook. On it I had pictures of the kind of work groups I imagined I would work with, images of a paper contract, dollar signs, golden keys, the words "Beliefs", "Success", "Service", "Contracts", "$8K", photos of a famous business woman, and a professional photo of myself.

Each day I wrote out my goal, using REPETITION to imprint it into my conscious and subconscious mind, daily building my internal belief. I wrote out a description of the type of work I would do, the feelings I would have, what I would see, smell, taste and touch. I used my Image-screen to visualize and describe in detail what it would be like. Here are some examples of what I said:

"I see myself as a valuable part of a team; interacting well with others, sharing ideas and making progress on worthwhile projects. I feel so excited to use my natural talents and abilities of training, designing training, speaking and coaching and be paid well for providing a great service to great people."

"I am happy to be a trainer and people champion. I am positive and optimistic each day and bring positive energy to the work environment. I am a person other people like to be around. I care deeply about the project and the people and love to get things done with quality and energy."

After writing out these descriptions, I closed my eyes and continued to IMAGE what I had written coming true. I knew holding the focus on the vision for two minutes is a magic amount of time to imprint it successfully onto my subconscious mind. The key is to hold the

continued

thought without any contradiction or resistance. Pure thought focused on the pleasure of the vision I have defined.

Next, I said out loud my personal declarations for all areas of my life including the statements that described the new contracts I wanted. With SOUND and passion and conviction I made these declarations over and over every single day. Next, I wrote out three areas each day for which I was grateful. I knew gratitude was the fastest way to feel good and keep my EMOTION at a high vibration level. I had the discipline to make this **RISE** process a daily ritual and loved doing it.

One day, after being diligent with the **RISE to Success** formula for a couple of months, I received a message "out of the blue" from a recruiter who found me on LinkedIn. He wanted to know if I would be interested in a contract position as a training specialist with Amway Global. They were moving a Nutrilite manufacturing plant from California to Washington State where I was living. It was three hours away, but they would pay a generous hourly rate plus travel, food and living expenses.

We scheduled a Skype interview, then two other interviews with leaders at Amway Global who were at their headquarters in Michigan. I was hired for the assignment and received $8,000/month, just as I had requested, and enjoyed it tremendously.

Remember, we become what we think about most of the time. And our subconscious mind does not know the difference between what is real or made up. Therefore when I vividly imagined the future work experience, in neurological terms it had taken place, and my brain gradually began to perceive it as real. With time, and two months of committed and persistent action, the experience I desired had manifested into reality. Imagine how exhilarating it will be for you when things come into your life just as you imagined they would!

In the following chapters in Part 4 we will break down the REPETITION - IMAGES - SOUND - EMOTION into specific "how-to" techniques and give you examples to follow. In this chapter on preparation, you will learn specifically how to use the **RISE to Success Journal**.

Preparation for the RISE to Success Journal

Let's get your materials together and put your brain in the best state possible to **RISE**:

Segment A: Material Preparation

1. Journal
2. Blue ink pen
3. Declarations
4. Audio recordings
5. Technology applications
6. Vision images

Segment B: Brain Preparation

1. Meditation
2. Prayer
3. Breathing

Segment A: Material Preparation

1. Journal

RISE to Success Journal: You can download a *free copy* of the daily form to make your own journal under "Free Gifts" at www.patrice-lynn.com. You can also order a pre-made journal and RISE to Success Journal Mini Course under "Products" at www.patricelynn.com.

2. Blue Ink Pen

For optimal results, you will write by hand in your journal with blue ink. WHA–A-AT? This may be surprising to you, but when you complete your daily entries don't use a computer. Writing by hand helps to build the neural patterns in your brain you need to achieve your goals.

The hand has a unique relationship with the brain when it comes to composing thoughts and ideas; cursive writing helps train the brain to integrate visual, and tactile information, and fine motor dexterity. More neuromuscular connections are activated with handwriting than typing, which strengthens your desired results.

Interesting, huh? We do live in a computer world with most forms of communication being typed, keyed or swiped these days. To tell you the truth, I was concerned about this fact when the **RISE** idea came to me. I thought, "Who will want to write things by hand? Everyone uses computers these days. I am going to have to create an app for this . . ." which struck me as an insurmountable task and I actually let it slide for quite some time. Isn't it startling how we can *all* find excuses to put our dreams on hold?

I had talked myself out of bringing these concepts to market and then two years later a very wealthy businessman exposed me to something incredible. *Did you know the wealthiest people in the world consistently write things down by hand*? They rarely use computers, although the people that work for them certainly do. Immediately I thought of a personal friend who became *extremely* wealthy who always had a yellow legal pad filled with handwritten notes. I also heard Wayne Dyer say he wrote all of his books by hand and then had them published. Also, General Douglas MacArthur hand wrote his autobiography nonstop. Handwriting uses more of your brain and is the preferred method for **RISE to Success.**

Now, about the blue ink: the vibrational energy of the color blue is a very creative energy. As you look at your handwritten goal in blue ink, it has more impact than using a different color — like black. You may think this is odd, but put it to the test and see for yourself.

TIP
Best way to program your brain is to write with blue Ink on white paper

On the visible light spectrum, blue is a high vibration color. It has a much higher vibrational frequency than black or red. Writing on white paper with blue ink imprints your goals and dreams further into your psyche and your memory.

3. Declaration Statements

These are the sentences or phrases you will say out loud to program your brain for success in the SOUND section of **RISE**. They may be handwritten or typed on separate pieces of paper; these are not recreated every day. You will want to amass a few lists of declarations for different moods and for variety. You may reproduce some of the examples listed in the Appendix or you can download a complimentary copy at www.patricelynn.com.

4. Audio Recordings

There are a many choices on the market of guided meditations, subliminal messages, relaxing music and hemi-sync technologies that synchronize the left and right brain. They are used to help you relax, visualize, de-stress, and manifest. I have some of my favorites from other people, and some I created as well in the resource sections. I also created an audio **RISE to Success Journal** Mini Course you can use to facilitate the daily journal process. All the details are available at www.patricelynn.com.

5. Technology Apps

In our fabulous high tech world, there is an app for everything today. ThinkUp is a free app designed to customize your own affirmations or pull from others. MindMovies is a paid app with a selection of images that can be put to music. You select the images that match your vision and produce your own short mental movie.

6. Collages or Vision Boards

A vision board is typically a large poster board with images from magazines cut out and glued to the board. A collage of visual images of what you want to manifest is an excellent way to continually program your subconscious mind and your RAS (reticular activation system). As you look at your vision frequently you will keep telling your brain what you want. This will work hand-in-hand with the **RISE to Success Journal** practice.

Once you have your materials together it is time to learn how to relax your brain.

Segment B: Brain Preparation

There are 3 practices you can do to prepare your brain wave state. They include meditation, prayer and breathing. You are the one who will choose which one, or which combination you will do each day to slow down your brain wave frequency. And you will also choose how long you will do them. These daily practices can range from 2 minutes to 2 hours; it all depends on how much time you are willing and able to spend doing these activities.

In the **RISE to Success Journal** process you will write your goals, your vision, and your gratitude list, as well as to speak out your declarations daily. The best way to do this is to drop into a more relaxed brain wave state so that what you want drops into your body-mind-spirit.

Brain Wave Frequencies Defined

As mentioned earlier in the book, our brain emits energy vibration or frequency. We all have four main brain wave electrical patterns, or frequencies, measured in cycles per second or hertz (Hz). Each brain wave pattern has its own set of characteristics that represent a specific level of brain activity and a unique state of consciousness. Let's review each brain state for a general understanding:

Beta 14-100 HZ - Normal everyday, conscious waking state

- Optimal daily functioning: conscious mind is aware and work is productive
- Low level functioning: over stressed with overactive "high beta" or fight/flight

Alpha 8-14 HZ - Relaxed state, first layer of subconscious

- Breath slows down, thoughts quiet down
- More relaxed and comfortable

Theta 4-7 HZ - REM sleep state, with open door to subconscious

- Conscious thought discontinues, deeper awareness
- Can become drowsy, more intuitive access to "Infinite Intelligence"

Delta 0.1-4 HZ - Dreamless sleep state, with open door to subconscious

- Slow, long brain waves
- High levels of access to the quantum field

Daily Practices to Relax and Prepare Your Brain

1. Meditation

The purpose of meditation is to slow down your brain waves and get beyond the thinking, analytical mind. When we meditate we can enter the subconscious and set positive intentions and change our unwanted programs. There are thousands of ways to meditate and many resources to help you as mentioned in the resource section.

2. Prayer

Prayer is when you talk to God, when you lift your thoughts up to the heavens, step out of the everyday world and access the divine. Prayer can bring peace and rest. Dozens of studies have found changes before and after prayer or meditative activities in the autonomic nervous system, which controls relaxation and arousal. Biological changes include decreased heart rate, blood pressure, and respiration. The real reason to do either meditation or prayer is because it resonates with you.

3. Breathing

The simplest way to transition from beta or alpha to theta is to focus on your breath. The breath and mind work in tandem, so as breath lengthens, your brain waves will slow down. Lucky for all of us in this fast-paced world, this can happen in a very short time. I suggest you breathe mindfully for two minutes. Everyone, no matter how "busy" can do 2 minutes. And remember, the total time it takes to **RISE** is 15 minutes per day.

I won a fascinating book at a business event, and I know it came to me via the quantum field so I could share this powerful and relevant information with you. The book is *Search Inside Yourself*, written by Chade-Meng Tan, Google's Chief Happiness Officer. Google has incorporated mindfulness training into their company culture and many have reported becoming better leaders and gaining promotions using these skills. Tan instituted mindfulness training at Google, and breath work is a key component of this training.

In his book Chade-Meng Tan says, "When you put your attention intensely on the breath, you are fully in the present for the duration of the breath. To feel regretful, you need to be in the past; to worry, you need to be in the future. Hence, when you are fully in the present, you are temporarily free from regret and worry." He goes on to explain how mindful breathing releases a heavy burden from the body and mind.

Chade-Meng Tan starts his attendees in this sold out program with 1-2 minutes of breath work and works up to longer periods. However, he relays that one Google VP found she got benefit in as little as 6 seconds with one deep mindful breath before walking into every meeting. I wanted to share this story to convince you that even two minutes of focused, mindful breathing will prepare you to enter into your **RISE to Success** morning ritual.

Let's RISE Together

Okay, are you ready to **RISE** to new heights in your life? Are you ready to bring more joy, happiness, opportunities, resources and magnificent people your way? Are you ready to shift into a positive high gear and experience success beyond your wildest dreams? Then let's move along in this process to the REPETITION- IMAGES - SOUND - EMOTION entries in your daily **RISE to Success Journal.** In the next chapters you receive specific examples to follow and you will have all the details you need to make this work for you. *I am excited for you.*

RISE to Success Journal: You can download a *free copy* of the daily form to make your own journal under "Free Gifts" at www.patricelynn.com. You can also order a pre-made journal and **RISE to Success Journal** Mini Course under "Products" at www.patricelynn.com.

16 How to RISE with REPETITION

"Choose your thoughts wisely because they create your reality."
— Patrice Lynn

With RISE You Can Achieve Your Goals More Easily and With Less Stress

With daily REPETITION and entries into the **RISE to Success Journal**, new patterns in your subconscious brain will be ingrained deeply, as opposed to simply thinking about or writing down goals once and then forgetting about them.

This is contrary to how I used to set goals when I first started out in my twenties.

I would write down on a paper "Go skiing at Zermatt in Switzerland, Earn $200,000/year, Have a home featured in magazine" then I would file the paper away and not even think about these goals. And you guessed it . . . they never happened.

If you do not focus on what you want frequently with passion and persistence, and see and feel yourself achieving it, then it will dissipate, and likely not materialize. When you take consistent action to write down in your journal what you want everyday, you will be taking the steps to turn your thoughts into matter. Your thoughts will literally create your life.

Repeating your goals every day in writing is a way to mentally imprint your deepest heart's desires. How long and how often you think these thoughts will impact you greatly as your beliefs change and become more positive. Numerous wealthy and influential people speak about writing, reading and seeing their goals every day as a way to impress the message into their mind.

Most People Don't Know What They Really Want

As I shared earlier, most people cruise along through life not knowing what they want. They are directionless, allowing themselves to be influenced by pop culture and people around them. Surprisingly, many people are much clearer about what they DON'T WANT than they are about what they DO WANT. Here are some examples:

What You DON'T WANT

- I don't want to be sick all the time.
- I don't want any more bills.
- I don't want another failed startup.
- I don't want a people on my board who don't understand my vision.
- I don't want to be so overweight.
- I don't want a girlfriend who argues with me.
- I don't want a controlling business partner who micromanages everything.

Many people actually don't *believe* they can actually have what they want, so they go through life much more focused on what they don't want. The good news about this situation is being clear about what you don't want will help you identify what you do want. The idea is to take the intense negative emotion you feel about each situation and channel that into empowering energy to get what you want.

Let's take each one of the previous **Don't Wants** and rephrase them into goals you can put into the **RISE to Success Journal**.

What You DO WANT

- I want to find an exercise partner to workout with.
- I want to generate 3 new clients.
- I want to find a business that plays to my strengths.
- I want to powerfully communicate my business vision.
- I want to be lean and feel younger.
- I want communication that just flows with my girlfriend.
- I want a partner who is excellent at delegating.

> "The more you focus on and talk about what you do want, the faster you will manifest your dreams and goals."
> — Stephen R. Covey

Take the Time to Write Down What YOU WANT

The key is to really take the time to find a quiet place to identify what you want to BE in your life, DO in your life, and HAVE in your life . . . and then write it down. Here is a start:

BE – Character qualities you want to possess: integrity, discipline and likability

_____

_____

_____

_____

DO - Actions and experiences: earn money, build a business, learn new skill, travel

_____

_____

_____

_____

HAVE - Material possessions, relationships, and fulfillment: peace of mind, exciting marriage, Mercedes sports car, new granite counter-tops, Master's degree, $_____

_____

_____

_____

_____

I love to share what I learned along the way about the BE-DO-HAVE principle. It is easy for anyone to think, "If only I could HAVE a million dollars, then I could DO what I want, and I would BE happy." When in reality, the BE is what comes first. Once you work on your character qualities, and then DO necessary actions and behaviors, then you can HAVE what you desire. Remember the lottery winner story from Chapter 7? Winning the lottery did not lead to happiness. Happiness (BE-ing) comes first. Remember the order of BE-DO-HAVE and identify these areas for yourself and you will be on your way.

TIP
Focus on What YOU WANT and Believe You Can Get It

As you spend time in these areas, you will generate inspiring ideas from which to choose your goals for the **RISE to Success Journal**.

Daily RISE to Success Action

Write down 3 goals everyday of what YOU WANT:

- Identify 3 things you want to focus on each day.
- Build frequency, intensity and duration as you think about them.
- With REPETITION you will program your brain for positive results.

As you write down your goals in blue ink on white paper, make sure to keep in mind the 3 guidelines for how to set a goal in Chapter 10: "Three Powerful Ingredients to Align Goals to Your Sweet Spot". The Sweet Spot is something you want that provides high excitement, gets you motivated, makes you feel good when you think about it, and is something you really believe you can attain: Passion — Possible — Positive Vibes.

3 Ways to Set a Goal

1. very specific
2. general
3. feeling it generates

Look at these examples for a goal of greater health and wellbeing:

1. very specific: I will lose 10 pounds by December 31st
2. general: Join a gym and begin weight training
3. feeling it generates: When I lose weight I will feel lean, sexy and younger

Look at these examples for a goal of better business results:

1. very specific: New clients will increase my income $20,000 this month/quarter/year
2. general: Attend XYZ Industry convention and find new clients
3. feeling it generates: My business is growing and I feel fantastic

Now it is your turn. Enter 3 goals every day into you **RISE to Success Journal.**

Go ahead - what comes to mind right now?

_____

_____

_____

Daily Rituals Help You Stay Focused and Get Results

Positive habits are the hallmark of highly successful people. Habits are hardwired pathways in your brain that exist by repeating them over and over. You will make new neural connections as you learn new things and take new actions. When you have a daily practice to identify, decide, and write down your goals you create a neurological pattern in your brain - a neural net. This daily ritual will program your brain to achieve what you want.

TIP
You become what you think about over and over

"You are today where your thoughts have brought you. You will be tomorrow where your thoughts take you." — James Allen

RISE to Success Journal: You can download a _free copy_ of the daily form to make your own journal under "Free Gifts" at www.patrice-lynn.com. You can also order a pre-made journal and **RISE to Success Journal** Mini Course under "Products" at www.patricelynn.com.

17 How to RISE with IMAGES

How Do You Become Good at Visualizing? Practice.

As you practice vividly seeing IMAGES and holding them within your mind for longer and longer durations your skill level will increase. Just like working out in the gym, your mind becomes stronger through daily repetition of activity. Mastery happens as you mentally rehearse your vision and begin to realize solid results from doing the visualizations. The only limit is your imagination and commitment.

TIP

Creative imaging includes more than just visual

Every day you use your **RISE to Success Journal**, you can gradually build your ability to imagine a positive future. Earlier in Chapter 3: "IMAGES: Bring Vision Into Reality on Your Image-screen", I shared 4 Keys to make the magic work for you as you do your visualizations. Let's take these 4 Magic Keys and expand them with more practical detail.

Magic Key #1 – Define Your Vision Everyday In Sensually Rich Detail

The **RISE to Success** System is designed to give you daily opportunities to practice a process of creatively imagining the places, people, events and circumstances you desire.

V-A-K is a brain training term to represent the three main modalities of learning:

- Visual - Use your sense of sight to see pictures, images and movies.
- Auditory - Use your sense of hearing to listen to sounds.
- Kinesthetic - Use your sense of touch to feel tactile sensations, movement and emotions.

Visualizing is more than just cognitively thinking about an upcoming event. For example, when athletes use visualization, they truly feel the event take place in their mind's eye.

Here is an example of what an athlete might be imagining just before she ever runs a race:

She feels her forefoot pushing off the track, she hears her feet hitting the ground methodically, and she sees herself surging ahead of the competition. She feels her heart pumping. Energy surges through her body. She hits the runners "high." She pulls ahead of the competition and wins the race.

Here is an example of a coffee shop owner who imagines her new coffee shop long before it happens: A customer walks into a coffee shop and is instantly captivated by the rich, pure, aroma of coffee. They sit at a small bistro table with their friends and enjoy a delicious croissant with the buzz of happy conversation from other patrons gathered closely around them. The environment is filled with joy, high energy and even romance between the couple gazing into each other's eyes in the corner. The espresso machine hisses as the baristas connect heart to heart with people who are drawn to the shop's positive vibe.

Can you experience both examples in vivid detail as if you were there? That is the goal. You want to make it so real on your Image-screen that you could reach out and touch it. Use your imagination to bring it to life in a sensory-rich fashion. And as far as business ideas, if it captures your imagination, it will capture others as well.

Let me share with you some of my personal examples from my own **RISE to Success Journal:**

EXAMPLE A:

I am helping people heal and grow and flourish. I am speaking, training, designing training and reaching people online. My heart is happy. I am alive, alert, and I feel great. Reaching out locally in Sacramento, regionally in northern California, the west, and the world. The community I live in is perfect for me, and I am blessed beyond measure to have support and connections with others.

EXAMPLE B:

I love my team. We create incredible learning experiences and are design thinkers. We help people learn, create tangible results and success. We are great partners and work in synergy with more energy. Our meetings are super productive. We are focused on our agenda, listen well to each other and get things done quickly.

EXAMPLE C:

I am speaking far and wide entertaining audiences with my **RISE to Success** program. People are having "Ah-ha" moments and smiles light up all across the room. The atmosphere shifts to a higher energy and peace is present. Several people want to work with me on a more personal level and enroll in my adventure retreats. I feel elated.

Make it Sensually Rich On Your Image-Screen

Decide on a desired outcome:

Select an outcome to focus on for each day's visualization: a sale, a speech, a performance, a race, gathering, business revenue, a new home, or a fun family event.

Color in the details:

- Rendering a service.
- Delivering products you intend to give in return for the money you want to earn.
- Finishing the race in a new personal best time.
- Creating a dinner party where everyone toasts your fabulous meal.
- Meeting new like-minded friends who laugh at the same things you do.
- Catching a big fish at a gorgeous lake in the Rocky Mountains.
- Moving into a new one-level home with a pool.

Be creative! The more you practice, the easier the IMAGES will come.

Now it is time to write out your ideal VISION:

_____

_____

_____

_____

_____

_____

_____

Magic Key #2 – Play The Mind Movie On Your Image-Screen For 2 Minutes

Now it is time to do some *future dreaming* about your ideal VISION:

- Writing out the words takes 30-60 seconds and adds to focused time.
- Close your eyes and IMAGINE for 2 minutes.

Imagine your positive outcome as if experiencing it in the present moment. Bring the pictures to life as if watching a movie on a movie screen. . . . make the colors bright and indulge all your other senses. Feel in your body a full range of emotions and be very specific with them: gratitude, joy, worthiness, peace, security, fun, happiness, warmth, accomplishment, pride, or bliss. This part is important . . . you must really feel what it would be like to already have what you mentally picture. Use your emotions to bring your mental movie to life — *with energy*.

"If one advances confidently in the direction of his dreams, and endeavors to live the life which he has imagined, he will meet with a success unexpected in common hours."
— Henry David Thoreau

Magic Key #3 – Hold Your Focus On This And Nothing Else

Now it is time to focus intently on your Image-screen:

- Focus on this vision of your future as a movie on your internal movie screen.
- See it - feel it - touch it - taste it - hear it - smell it.
- Stay present - stay focused - hold onto it and return if you drift away.
- Stay with it until your 2 minutes is up and you can say – "Ah, I did it."

Magic Key #4 – Gradually Increase The Frequency, Duration And Intensity

Over time increase the energy of your ideal vision:

- Intensify your vision as you practice the RISE.
- Think about your vision frequently throughout the day.
- Increase the length of your IMAGE session by 1 minute at a time.
- Add some additional, deeper guided visualizations — see references.

> **TIP**
> Repeat this IMAGE process every day in your RISE TO SUCCESS JOURNAL

RISE to Success Journal: You can download a *free copy* of the daily form to make your own journal under "Free Gifts" at www.patrice-lynn.com. You can also order a pre-made journal and **RISE to Success Journal** Mini Course under "Products" at www.patricelynn.com.

Inspired Imagination is Greater Force Than Willpower

Over time in the field of personal development the concept of *willpower* has been touted as the way to make things happen in life. Lately there are more authorities speaking out against this as they agree willpower can be counter productive to activities like losing weight and achieving goals. They say trying to make something happen with effort, determination, and force does not always work and can be a negative way to break a bad habit or achieve an outcome. Perhaps a better approach comes from the inside out.

Dr. Maxwell Maltz said in his book, *Psycho-Cybernetics;* "Embracing new, good habits is sufficient to displace old bad habits without a struggle. Through imagination, a person can plant a new self-image in the subconscious mind. This new self-image acts automatically to guide the person to a goal — like on autopilot."

This is good news, isn't it? What is important for you to know is the new person you will become through your daily visualizations will help you to create any positive outcome you desire. Through repetition of IMAGES you will replace your old patterns of the subconscious with new patterns. Essentially it is like a magic eraser to remove the black marks of the past and overwrite them with new scripts. Ringing in the new will become much easier than struggling to stop doing the old.

"The true sign of intelligence is not knowledge but imagination."
— Einstein

RISE to Success Journal: You can download a *free copy* of the daily form to make your own journal under "Free Gifts" at www.patrice-lynn.com. You can also order a pre-made journal and **RISE to Success Journal** Mini Course under "Products" at www.patricelynn.com.

How to RISE with SOUND 18

Just like heavyweight boxing champion Muhammad Ali, the more you do your SOUND declarations on a daily basis, the more your confidence will grow. Just as he explained by his statement "I am not conceited, I am just convinced that I am the Greatest!"; as he kept winning, he was able to become bolder and bolder about his declarations.

REPETITION changes the inner thoughts from weak to strong, and eventually you will believe it as true. As you believe what you say, and speak it out frequently with intensity and power, it will activate the laws of nature. You, too, will become a *winner*.

TIP
State out loud your positive declarations and goals for more power

Make Your Declaration List

As you are working through your **RISE to Success** Journal, you will get to the SOUND section and this is when you speak your positive declarations out loud. What sources do you have to create an inspiring list of declarations you will use each day?

- Use any examples in this book (see Appendix)
- Let your intuition guide you to create your own
- Search online for positive declarations or affirmations
- Make more than one list for variety

Store Your Declaration List

Whether you decide to make your own journal, purchase a pre-made **RISE to Success Journal**, or buy or create a **RISE to Success Workbook**, you will need a separate place to store the lists of declarations. Which of these ideas do you like the best?

- Notebook or 3-ring binder
- Typed page taped to your wall/mirror for frequent viewing
- Typed page carried in your purse or wallet
- Note app on your phone

Speak Your Declaration List

SOUND: Daily spoken declarations help you attract into your life all the love, appreciation, success, and abundance you desire and deserve. Not only that, but daily positive declarations will also allow you to recreate your self-image, replace your limiting beliefs, and **RISE** up to a higher energetic vibration. Speak out your list of declarations with passion and enthusiasm as you do your daily **RISE to Success**.

You are welcome to speak your declarations several times a day. The best time to **RISE** is when you wake up, and also wonderful to do just before you go to sleep. These are open windows to the subconscious mind at these times.

The more you speak the declarations, the more often you will focus your imagination on the mental image of your life vision. Every time you focus your words on your vision, it becomes clearer. Every thought has an image. All of the steps of **RISE to Success** work synergistically together:

REPETITION: The thoughts you think over and over that become automatic
IMAGES: The sensory rich images you see in a your mind's eye
SOUND: The words you speak and the sound vibrations they emit
EMOTION: Feelings you feel that radiate positive or negative energy

Speak WHAT YOU WANT, not WHAT YOU DON'T WANT

The thoughts we exercise the most are the easiest ones to think. That also applies to the words we speak. *The words we speak the most are the easiest ones to speak.* Listen to what you are saying at all times. Catch yourself when you speak low vibration words of lack and loss and frustration and disappointment:

- "I'm losing my mind."
- "I am so unlucky."
- "I never get a break."
- "I am too old to get a job."
- "I'm always getting sick."
- "I will never get out of debt."
- "I am way too busy." (Who made your schedule?)
- "I'm so lonely, bored, unhappy, discouraged . . ."

"Cancel — Cancel!!" As you catch yourself, immediately delete these words from your memory bank and from your vibration. Immediately overwrite with the positive. My friends and I catch ourselves when we slip up and we remind each other of the power of our words. We empower ourselves by passionately speaking out *what we do want*.

Remember, the energy vibration of words never ends because science tells us sound vibrations never end, they just dissipate. That means what you say has a lasting impact on your life. Instead of speaking negative, you can acknowledge your situation in a realistic way first and then move into more positive reframes at the end of the statement. Reframes = reality + positive expectation. Examples include:

- "I am not feeling that great today, but I know things are going to get better and better."
- "I had something go awry, and I choose to take responsibility that I create my own reality."
- "Lately I have had some tough things to deal with, and soon it will be much smoother sailing."

What to Say When You Are Out of Work or Out of Money . . . or Both

"This isn't going to be good news - today is your last day." And poof - you are unemployed. I know from past experience that sometimes you can just be so down and feel so hopeless that it is downright challenging to speak positive things about your life and situation. Can you relate? Life can throw us so many curve balls:

- What if your startup failed and you have to move on to another opportunity?
- What if you have to move and you are not sure where to go?
- What if you run out of money and aren't sure where the next cash will come from?
- What if you sold everything you own and now you need to find work so you can find a place to live?
- What if you just got let go from a job?

My friend and sought-after international speaker and consultant, Troy McClain from the 1st season of *The Apprentice* offers a valuable positive reframe. He suggests using this phrase when in those transition times: "I am in between success cycles". Now isn't that uplifting? With this declaration, you are focusing on the good things to come and what you *want* to happen next in your life. By saying this phrase you are not wallowing in the gutter and lamenting your position in life. You are preparing for the positive success you have yet to experience.

Hearing Troy's idea, I came up with my own at a time when I really needed a new perspective. To reframe and remind myself of the good things to come I say: "I am uniquely positioned for my next great opportunity" Saying these words just downright feels good. Maybe you will want to try it.

I Am Who I Say I Am

The two most powerful words in the English language are "I AM". Whatever you say after those two words will be programmed into your mind and heart. How do I know this is so powerful? Well, first of all, in the best selling book of all time, the bible, God said, "I AM THAT I AM". The spoken word, especially following "I AM" is extremely powerful to create the life we want because we are made in God's image. We are designed to be co-creators of our lives.

> "Whatever follows I AM will come looking for you."
> — Joel Osteen, Pastor and Motivational Speaker

I AM beautiful, a masterpiece, terrific, destined for greatness, one of a kind, valuable, youthful, vibrant, confident, secure, excited about my future, favored everywhere I go.

What kind of I AM's are coming out to your mouth?? Make sure they are positive.

Examples:

- I am expecting something good to happen to me today.
- I am an unstoppable entrepreneur.
- I am winning everyday in every way.
- I am attracting rich and loving relationships.
- I am fully alive and happy.
- I am excited to see my bank accounts increase dramatically.
- I am positive and optimistic about life.
- I am full of energy, motivated and committed to achieve my goal.

It Works When You *Believe* It

Some people have negative associations with affirmations because they are saying statements they don't actually believe. Make sure you are able to *believe* what you are saying, and therefore the SOUND that is coming out of your mouth.

In Alex Loyd's book *The Love Code*, he states that research was done to prove when we say an affirmation and we don't believe it, it becomes a negative instead of a positive, and we are really hurting ourselves. Loyd says, "For about a year and a half I tested affirmations in my practice with the heart rate variability test (the medical test for stress). What I found was that when people said affirmations that they did not believe, their stress level spiked. Well, stress is how they got the problem in the first place. So in reality, they were trying to solve their stress problem with something that was causing more stress." Loyd goes on to say, ". . . in order to be effective, the person has to believe the affirmation". I found his research fascinating.

This could explain some of the pushback about doing this activity, with some people saying, "Affirmations don't work!" I say, reframe them to "declarations", use the following tweaks, and listen to your heart. Use the structure of the **RISE to Success Journal** as a positive touchstone for you.

How to Turn a Declaration Into Something You Believe

Since affirmations have to be *believable* to be effective, I have gathered some "start-up" statements, or "tweaks" to adapt the statement and turn it into something with a positive impact for you. I have learned it truly helps to put some qualifying words in front of the declaration. Some examples of words you can use to make the statements more believable are:

"Tweaks" - Reword with these phrases to make statements feel better and be more believable to your subconscious mind:

I love how it feels when _____

I have decided to be _____

More and more _____

I love the idea of _____

I am excited about _____

I love seeing myself _____

Soon, I will _____

Examples of Declarations with positive tweaks:

- **More and more** I AM positive and optimistic about life!
- **I AM excited about** having ____ customers/clients getting fantastic results.
- **I love seeing myself** fully alive and happy.
- **I have decided to be** an excellent money manager.
- **I love how it feels when** I AM relaxed and productive.
- **I love how it feels when** I make excellent business decisions.
- **It excites me** to have a well functioning body.

If you don't feel it is accurate to say, "I am an excellent money manager", for instance, because you are just terrible at managing your money; you are late on bills, you spend more than you take in, etc. etc. Your brain will be like a person with their arms crossed in defiance saying, "I don't think so!" Your brain will just not let it in.

Yet if you really, really want to be better at managing your money, well then just add the tweak and say out loud "**I have decided to be** an excellent money manager." And then you can add, "**I am excited** to see my bank accounts increase dramatically" and/or, "Money flows to me easily and frequently." (One of my personal favorites)

Can you imagine how much better this will feel than the old, outdated instructions some us have heard about saying "affirmations" in the positive tense as if it is happening now — whether or not it is even remotely true?

Examples: "I am a millionaire", "I drive a Rolls Royce", and "I live in Thailand" when you actually have a net worth of $100,000, drive a Subaru and live in Denver. I have found these new types of statements with the tweaks to be like *a breath of fresh air* and very easy to believe, which is the KEY to having them come true! Remember, we must find our Sweet Spot — the intersection of *what we want* with *what we believe is possible*.

Here are a couple positive statements with tweaks I say often:

- I am excited to see my bank accounts increase dramatically
- More and more people want to work with me
- Soon, I will earn $_____/month passive income to pay for my desired lifestyle

My confidence grows as I speak out words I believe and can easily imagine happening. Wouldn't you love this as well? Try it out today.

Another excellent "tweak" for declarations comes from Bob Proctor. Proctor is widely regarded as one of the living masters and teachers of "The Law of Attraction" and is featured in the blockbuster hit movie, *The Secret*. He is a bestselling author, business consultant and life mentor. Bob's tweak for declarations goes at the beginning of the sentence:

"I am so happy and grateful now that . . ." (Fill in the blanks with anything you desire).

Bob Proctor also has a more complete version that he believes is the most powerful statement to say on a regular basis. "I am so happy and grateful now that money is coming to me in increasing amounts, through multiple sources, on a continuous basis." Bob Proctor is considered one of the world's foremost wealth coaches. He is a multi-millionaire and still going strong teaching and traveling the world in his 80s.

When you have a list of all the things you are doing to create financial freedom in your life, all the wealth in the quantum field picks up on that vibration. Money responds to your energetic voice in a positive way, moving in your direction. The more you think and talk about good, positive things the more you will see them happening.

List of Popular Affirmations

- "I am grateful for the good things in my life."
- "I believe in myself. I have the ability to succeed."
- "The more I focus my mind on the good, the more good comes into my life."
- "I love myself, respect myself, and accept myself exactly as I am."
- "I accept myself and know that I am worthy of great things in life."
- "I deserve to be happy and loved."
- "I can accomplish anything I set my mind to."
- "I am releasing all the negative emotions from my system."
- "I am willing to step out of my comfort zone."
- "I am letting go of all my worries and fears."

Are You Speaking Into Cultural Norms?

A huge area we all must be aware of is negative, low vibration comments emanating from our culture. These include media, government, arts and entertainment, education, healthcare, family, and business. This is rampant in our social media sharing society today. Everyone has an opinion and many want to express the negative, mostly because it is a habit. And you can easily find people to commiserate with. Before you speak, can you ask yourself: "Will my words help anyone or will they just add to the negativity already out there?"

It is an easy trap to fall into — to talk negatively about people and current events. Please pay attention and keep it positive so you rise up as a leader and do not stay at a lower vibration with the masses. Notice the vibe you feel when you hear:

- "Hollywood is a mess."
- "Our President is an idiot."
- "Our economy is never going to turn around."
- "Schools are ruining our kids."
- "Global warming is going to kill us all."
- "Health care is going down the tubes."

Decide To Be Influential Instead Of Popular

The most successful people I know never make these types of comments listed above. They only make statements about the changes they want to make in our world that will make it a better place. Instead of joining into negative banter, they know deep down their words are powerful. They know what they say can also determine how they feel, as well as impact others around them. They don't want to feel bad and turn off the flow of good things coming to them. Here are some examples of statements that I have heard influential people make:

- "My kids and I are going on a mission trip to build a home for a family in Mexico."
- "I am investing in companies that will take actions to better our planet, as well as focus on profits — the truly conscious companies."
- "As a family, we are committed to home school our children even though it is a big time and energy commitment."

While at a Dream Conference in Lake Tahoe with over 500 people, I personally spoke with Brad Cummings, Executive Producer of the movie, *The Shack*. The book was quite controversial because it portrayed God and the Holy Spirit as unconventional people (Black woman and Asian woman respectively.) Cummings took a stance to be influential instead of popular and bring the film to market in Hollywood. This was amid much opposition from production companies that did not buy into his belief in its mass appeal. He chose to personally invest to see it through to completion. The film, which was released in the winter of 2017, has grossed $100 million in revenue worldwide. Cummings shared with us the positive declaration he spoke out loud, with passion, to bring his dream into reality:

- "My new screenplay will impact Hollywood with the power of its message."

There are many stories such as this one and others I have told in the book that reinforce the power of SOUND declarations to shape our future reality. Positive words filled with intention bring about the events, circumstances and opportunities we desire.

In conclusion, here are some reminders for what you have learned about SOUND:

- Words have creative power to bless or curse your future.
- If you criticize your future, you are against yourself — *Be for yourself.*
- Use your words to bless your future — *Be uplifting.*
- Life and death are in the power of the tongue.
- Words have sound frequency that affects physical matter.
- Change on the inside before change on the outside happens.

RISE to Success Journal: You can download a *free copy* of the daily form to make your own journal under "Free Gifts" at www.patrice-lynn.com. You can also order a pre-made journal and **RISE to Success Journal** Mini Course under "Products" at www.patricelynn.com.

19 How to RISE with EMOTION

How would you like an abundance of practical ideas in which to bring positive, feel good emotions into your life? You can use them throughout every day. Remember, the intention is to generate "Good, Good, Good - Good Vibrations" just like the famous Beach Boy's song.

Let's recap the **RISE to Success** process once again:

- Use REPETITION to think about what you want over and over.
- Craft IMAGES to bring your vision to life in a sensually rich mental movie.
- Speak and say words to generate SOUND vibrations that declare what you want.
- Pay attention to your EMOTIONS to feel good, more and more of the time.

It takes discipline to spend the 15 minutes a day to fill in all of your **RISE** entries. When you do the EMOTION gratitude part, you will learn to be happy, feel content and satisfied with your life. You will feel good because you are focused on what you already have, not what you don't have. You can start your day off on a positive note as you enter three things for which you are grateful.

> "If you look at what you have in life, you'll always have more. If you look at what you don't have in life, you'll never have enough." — Oprah Winfrey

Gratitude is the Fast Track to Positive Vibes

Being grateful for a variety of things in your life *every day* is the quickest way to feel really good *right now*. This technique is so simple and works instantly because you cannot possibly feel "bad" when you are thinking about what you are grateful for and writing it down. This is the exact reason I created the **RISE to Success Journal.** Now you have the perfect place to express your appreciation for life every day.

Here is a contrast between being grateful and feeling good vs. feeling bad. The point is made here that you will attract into your life what you are sending out. Remember the brain is like a radio transmitter sending and receiving energy frequencies:

- If you put out a vibration of "how lucky I am, how blessed I feel, how thankful I am, how lucky I feel, how appreciative I am" you will receive more of what you are feeling.
- If you put out a vibration of anger, "I am so frustrated, errr - that makes me mad!" then events, circumstance and people that make you feel more of the same will come into your life.

Can you see how important it is to keep your emotions at a higher level?

In the RISE Journal you will simply write out three areas each day for which you are grateful. Every day without fail, the "attitude of gratitude" will serve you to the highest level. This is the fastest way to get yourself feeling good and keeps your EMOTION at a high vibration level. Go ahead — what comes to mind? "I am thankful for . . ."

- People
- Places
- Material items
- Feelings
- Future events
- Opportunities
- Circumstances
- Creative ideas
- Wins

_____

_____

_____

As promised, I will help you to learn gratefulness by giving you several good ideas and categories from which to pull your three daily gratitude entries.

People Gratitude: You can be grateful for certain people in your life: friends, family, colleagues, teachers and mentors (some of whom you've met and some you know only through their books, videos or media appearances). Insert a name in the underlined areas below.

- Meeting <u>a new friend</u>
- <u>Person</u> who encouraged me today
- <u>Conference attendee</u> I met
- <u>Mechanic</u> who serviced my car
- Call from <u>my mother</u>
- <u>Homeless person</u> I gave $1 to
- <u>Executive</u> who took my call
- <u>Colleague</u> in my mastermind group
- <u>Girlfriend/boyfriend</u> I enjoy so much
- Wonderful, loving <u>spouse</u>
- Learning from a certain <u>teacher</u>

"The deepest craving of human nature is the need to be appreciated" — William James

Due to quantum entanglement and the fact that we are all one, we are all connected — when you appreciate someone in your life, what are the chances they can feel it on an energetic level? Interesting question to ponder, isn't it . . .

Things Gratitude: Be grateful for things in your life like a warm, cozy bed, an invigorating shower or a piece of art that brings you joy.

- Hip sunglasses
- Heated neck pillow my friend made
- Green shake - world's best fast food
- My wok from china town San Diego
- My vehicle
- Favorite computer case or bag
- Tea cup for morning tea
- Sun-filled room
- Insightful movie
- Cell phone
- Fresh veggies from the garden
- Crisp apple

Activity Gratitude: Some days it is a speech you gave and the people who were inspired by it. Maybe it is even a quote you read that reminded you of who you are and your destiny, or putting on your favorite perfume or after-shave.

- Going on a walk
- Eating a meal with special friends
- Making connections on social media
- The ability to think of things I am thankful for
- Drinking fine wine
- Cooking my favorite dish
- Learning new things

Nature Gratitude: Nature is filled with things for which to be grateful: a red cardinal in the tree outside, a rainbow after a storm or watching light, fluffy snowflakes ascend softly from the sky. Sunrises and sunsets happen everyday. Some take your breath away and others you can appreciate because you are alive to see another day. There is always something to appreciate.

- Brilliant orange and pink skies
- Green grass
- Waterfalls

- The sounds of a rushing creek
- A stately oak tree
- Sighting a rare tarantula
- Eagles and hawks soaring
- Lime green aspen trees in the spring
- The sound of migrating geese
- Roses in bloom that smell heavenly

Feeling Gratitude: You can even focus your gratitude on feelings as you experience them. The power and intensity of these positive feelings will increase the more frequently you do this activity. *That is why **RISE** is designed to do everyday.* You can also do it 2x/day, each morning and evening. There is room in the **RISE to Success Journal** for both entries.

- I feel terrific
- Thank you, I am feeling so great
- My body feels strong
- I feel so lucky
- Wow, I am so blessed
- I feel at peace
- I feel so happy
- I am so excited about life
- My life is filled with wonder

Happiest People Reminder: Even in the remote tribes of Ethiopia, Africa, many of the people are very happy there because they have learned to enjoy the simple pleasures of life: water to drink, rice to eat and a new baby being born. A smile from a friend and a good night's sleep nestled next to loved ones brings great joy. Whoever you are, wherever you are, there is something to be grateful for.

The **RISE to Success Journal** is available to make this easier for you. As you contemplate what you are grateful for your EMOTIONAL STATE will rise in frequency and you will feel better than you did before you started the process. You will look forward to do this every day and before long you will realize you are feeling better every day because *you have so much to be thankful for.* What you focus on grows and expands.

RISE to Success Journal: You can download a *free copy* of the daily form to make your own journal under "Free Gifts" at www.patrice-lynn.com. You can also order a pre-made journal and **RISE to Success Journal** Mini Course under "Products" at www.patricelynn.com.

Future Accomplishments: Another very powerful and effective way to give thanks is for the things you want in the future. "Thank you for the opportunity to. . . ."

- Sing the star-spangled banner in front of millions.
- See my screenplay turned into a movie in theaters.
- Write a bestseller book.
- Have my song recorded by RCA/BMG records.
- Be on a national news show talking about my book.
- Meet a famous celebrity.
- Meet influential people who will open doors for me.
- Design and build my own home.
- Conduct successful retreats in Sedona, Arizona.

You can tap into the feelings you *will have* when you accomplish specific results and experience special circumstances and events. This will bring even more clarity about what you want into your atmosphere as well as lift your vibration and energy frequency.

Earlier in the book in Chapter 5: "EMOTION: Feel Good to Pull Positive Results To You Quickly" it was suggested you can also remember very positive mountaintop experiences you have had in the past. The intention is to tune into those "feel good memories" and layer new future accomplishments onto those positive feelings.

Daily Rituals Help You To Stay In A Positive State Of Mind And Heart

As you write down your gratitude list you will immediately start vibrating at a higher level of energy frequency. And remember, the higher your frequency, the more quickly you will draw to you the circumstances, events and people who will help you to get the results you want in business and life.

"Thank You" Will Immediately Help Everyone To FEEL GOOD NOW

Throughout the day you can also keep the gratitude vibe going when you show sincere appreciation to waiters, grocery checkout clerks, printers, gas station attendants, and a variety of telephone customer service agents. A sincere, heartfelt *"Thank You"* such as:

- Thank you for helping me.
- Thank you for your excellent service.
- Thank you for answering my question.
- Thank you for being so well informed.
- Thank you for your superior positive attitude.
- Thank you for being a joy to work with.

As you consistently look for the good versus the negative or bad, you will maintain this higher vibration throughout your day. Soon, it will become a habit and your brain will be wired to search for the good in each and every situation. Imagine how *fantastic* this will make you *feel*, not to mention those people around you! People will be attracted to this positive energy that you will emanate everywhere you go. Smiles will come naturally. Think of yourself as a farmer sowing seeds of gratitude everywhere you go. Imagine the harvest that can come from planting so many good seeds.

Immediate Actions Shift Your Emotions to a Higher Level

Immediate action steps to improve your "vibe" can make a huge difference in your life. Once you are aware you are feeling down, discouraged, angry, fearful, resentful or hurt, you can take some immediate actions to feel better. Remember, it is about moving up the emotional scale, one or two steps at a time, with the goal of *feeling better*, not necessarily blissful.

Here are some suggestions:

- Exercise of any kind
- Go out into the sun
- Listen to uplifting music
- Dance
- Laugh
- Sing

- Cook
- Create something with your hands
- Watch an uplifting movie
- Eat a nutritious meal
- Hug someone
- Bounce on a rebounder
- Meditate
- Receive energy healing
- Take a bubble bath
- Get or give a massage
- Talk to a plant
- Pet a dog or cat
- Play a board game with friends
- Look at your vision board
- Play an instrument
- Count your blessings

You are responsible for your life, your thoughts, your feelings, your words, and your behaviors. As you become more self aware of what you are feeling, you can use these immediate actions to shift yourself up the emotional scale and begin to feel better.

TIP
Protein and complex carbs are the perfect fuel for your brain

In conclusion, the daily practice of gratitude will transform your life. Your perspective will change and the simple pleasures of life will take on greater significance. The small things will make you smile. You will begin to notice more and more to appreciate in your life. Bottom line — daily gratitude will feel *really good*.

RISE to Success Journal: You can download a *free copy* of the daily form to make your own journal under "Free Gifts" at www.patrice-lynn.com. You can also order a pre-made journal and **RISE to Success Journal** Mini Course under "Products" at www.patricelynn.com.

Conclusion

Are You Ready For a Life You Love?

Once you practice **RISE to Success** over and over, you will begin to experience powerful results from your actions. You will have developed a positive, life-giving skill that will pay off day after day, month after month, year after year for your lifetime.

This is a very simple process, and yet the impact it can have on your life is phenomenal. Einstein said, "Everything should be made as simple as possible, but not simpler." **RISE to Success** is basic and doable, yet to get the maximum impact requires a daily commitment. This may not be that easy . . . until it becomes a habit. At that point you will be like me, and not want to be without it. You will want your journal by your side wherever you go.

"Consistency is what turns the desire to change into success."
— Patrice Lynn

As you have learned, the science behind the **RISE** is sound and unlimited in its ability to bring to you the good things you want in your life. This process does work amazingly well for everyone who applies it. The principles of mental imagery, spaced repetition, neuroscience and quantum physics ensure you will have what you think, see, say, feel and do. Your intention and consciousness will create *results*.

Now you have in your hands the answers to how to utilize more of your brain potential. Your brain is a supercomputer of exponential proportions. No actual manmade computer compares to the abilities of your brain. Your brain processes 400 billion bits of information per second — yet you are aware of only about 2,000 bits of info per second that relate to your body, your environment and time. What could happen as you increase your awareness and control of your brain's processing ability?

Having a vision for your life and thinking about the future is a practical skill that primes your brain for greater creativity, optimism and adaptability to change. As we imagine the future we desire, the brain perceives it as if we are experiencing it in real time, collapsing time and bringing reality from the future to the present moment.

That means the capacity you have to reach into the supernatural realm and bring treasures forward into your life is astounding. You can call those things that are not as though they are — from energy into matter. The quantum field, vaster than the galaxies, will respond. Remember this every day. Never be limited by what you see and feel. There is so much more available to you. The universe is truly unlimited, abundant, plentiful and friendly.

"Few things are more powerful than a life lived with passionate clarity." — Patrice Lynn

---

Whatever you think and feel, you will produce more of — just like your trillions of cells multiplying every day in your body. This multiplication is great as long as you stay focused on what you *want*, instead of what you *don't want*. If you feel the urge to complain, feel bad, speak negative, be unkind, please recalibrate. As you keep your positive vibe up, the more positive will be drawn to you; like bees to honey, your life will gradually taste sweeter. Your energy affects everything around you. Change your energy and you will indeed change your life.

Personal Growth Can Set You Free

One of my deepest passions in life is personal growth. I didn't realize when I started on this path how much it was a self-serving career for me, literally life-saving. As I learned and taught others, I grew. As I challenged others to evolve, I did as well. I hope you will find, as I have, that it is fun to feel yourself grow more confident, more effective, more aware, and stronger — day-by-day, month-by-month, and year-by-year.

I truly dream of a day when people are set free from whatever holds them back from living the life they were born to live. My heart mourns for people who are suffering from physical, mental, emotional and spiritual maladies because I now know there are so many beautiful answers to these situations and challenges. Many people are close-minded, uneducated or unaware. They live in outdated paradigms of health, wellness and true prosperity. In my lifetime, I am inspired to change that for as many people as possible. For every person who is set free, my heart rejoices.

Give Your Best Self to the World

Life is a gift, and it offers us the privilege, opportunity, and responsibility to give something back by becoming more. What a noble cause in life to *be more*, to be our best self and give to the world the gifts and talents we were born to give. Nothing is more rewarding.

Knowing you're on the road to your definition of success and achievement is truly satisfying. Creating a life you love is the best kind of life to live. Now is your time, my friend. Be inspired. Dream. Be More. Be a Leader and step out further on this adventurous journey.

**RISE To The Challenge Like The Sun Rises In The Sky
And Brightens The Lives Of Others**

RISE to Success!

Patrice Lynn

References

Books

5 Second Rule — Mel Robbins
Becoming Supernatural — Dr. Joe Dispenza, PhD
Breaking The Habit Of Being Yourself — Dr. Joe Dispenza, PhD
Change Your Brain, Change Your Life — Dr. Daniel Amen, MD
Chicken Soup For The Soul Series — Jack Canfield and Mark Victor Hansen
Finding The Champion Within — Bruce Jenner
Happiness Advantage — Shawn Achor

Harry Potter Series — J.K. Rowling
I'll See It When I Believe It — Dr. Wayne Dyer, PhD
Jane Fonda's Workout — Jane Fonda
Keys To Take Your Quantum Leap — David Van Koevering
Peak Performance — Charles Garfield, PHD
Positive Imaging — Norman Vincent Peale
Psycho Cybernetics — Dr. Maxwell Maltz
Quantum Faith — Annette Capps
The Hidden Messages Of Water — Masaru Emoto
Search Inside Yourself — Chade-Meng Tan
Secrets Of The Millionaire Mind — T. Harv Eker
Soul Journeys — Rosalind McKnight
Switch On Your Brain — Dr. Caroline Leaf, PhD
The Answer — John Assaraf
The Biology Of Belief — Dr. Bruce H. Lipton, PhD
The Emotion Code — Dr. Bradley Nelson, DC
The Healing Code — Dr. Alexander Loyd, PhD, ND
The Heart Math Solution — Doc Childre and Howard Martin
The Love Code — Dr. Alexander Loyd, PhD, ND
The New Leadership Paradigm — Richard Barrett
The Secret — Rhonda Byrne
The Seven Habits Of Highly Effective People — Stephen R. Covey
The Shack — William P. Young
The Success Principles — Jack Canfield
The Supernatural Power Of A Transformed Mind — Bill Johnson
Think And Grow Rich — Napoleon Hill
Transformation Of The Inner Man — John Loren Sandford
Unlimited Power — Anthony Robbins
Who Switched Off My Brain — Dr. Caroline Leaf, PhD
Women With Swords — Lisa Bevere
You Can Have It All — John Assaraf
You Can Heal Your Life — Louise Hay

You Tube Channels

Brad Yates, guided EFT energy healing: "eftwizard"
Dr. Joe Dispenza, supernatural: "drjoedispenza"
John Assaraf, brain expert: "PraxisNowLLC"
Dr. Caroline Leaf, PhD, brain and quantum physics: "DrCarolineLeaf"

Movies

What the Bleep Do We Know — William Arntz, Betsy Chasse, Mark
   Vincent
The Secret — Rhonda Byrne
The Shack — Brad Cummings, Gil Netter

Appendix

RISE to Success Declarations

I talk positively about people, places and circumstances of my life, which keeps my vibration at a higher level, and attracts to me matching high vibration people, places and circumstances.

My thoughts are powerful! What I think about most of the time is what comes about in my life. Where my focus goes is where my energy flows.

When I think positive thoughts, happy brain chemicals are released in my brain and I feel good!

My thoughts RISE up, my feelings RISE up, my words RISE up, my actions RISE up and I generate more and more positive results in my life.

I choose my words carefully because my life obeys my words.

Success is the freedom to live my life in the way that I want.

As I RISE I am more and more successful, prosperous, healthy and happy.

My personal reality is created moment by moment by how I think and feel and what I say and do.

I love how it feels to tap into the quantum field of unlimited possibilities. Frequently, I experience my thoughts becoming something tangible and real.

The 60,000 thoughts I have a day are units of energy, which I use wisely to create a magnificent life.

Writing my goals down everyday activates my brain and body to remember them, and inspires my subconscious mind to work around the clock to make them a reality.

As I imagine a vision of my ideal future in vivid detail for 2 minutes a day, I wire my brain to RISE to higher and higher levels of success.

The sound vibration of the words I speak affects physical matter around me and draws to me things of equal vibration. As I speak positive, I attract more positive into my life.

When I walk into a room people immediately feel uplifted by the good vibrations I send out. I RISE and people RISE around me.

I am responsible to manage my feelings. The better and better I feel, my body becomes a magnet to what I desire.

When I change the way I feel, the situations around me change.

My dominant thoughts turn into beliefs that overcome my genetic programming. My internal environment is more powerful than my DNA. My future self is free, healthy, vibrant and alive!

I enthusiastically identify 3 things for which I am grateful every day to expand my emotional energy field and RISE to Success.

When I express gratitude for the things that I love and appreciate, more of the things I love an appreciate come into my life.

The universe is a great echo chamber that bounces back to me what I send out.

I use my mind to design a life I love.

I see and feel abundance coming to me.

I speak of my future success. I am eternally grateful for all that I am.

I turn up my productivity as I rewire and retrain my brain to a new level. Higher levels of productivity produce the positive results I want.

Repetition is the key to becoming the person I want to be.

The more new healthy networks I build in my brain, the more intelligent and prosperous I become.

Everyday I declare positive statements over my life, and day-by-day they become true.

I am a master of my life — I RISE up everyday and tune my brain vibrations to design my ideal day. Repetition day after day creates my ideal life.

I am excited about having the power to create anything I want with my mind — this is how I RISE to Success

Positive Declarations

I believe something good is going to happen to me today!

I am full of energy, motivated and committed to achieve my goals.

I am grateful for the good things in my life.

I create my life. I create the exact amount of my financial success.

I live a prosperous and enjoyable life.

I have what it takes!

I can accomplish anything I set my mind to.

I am passionate about using my gifts to help others.

I am letting go of all my worries and fears.

I am a powerful manifestor.

The phone rings often with people who recognize my talent.

Money comes to me easily and frequently.

I am a valuable member of a team, family and community.

I have a positive attitude about life.

I deserve to be happy and loved.

I accept myself and know that I am worthy of great things in life.

I am a person other people love to be around.

I believe in myself. I have the ability to succeed.

The more I focus my mind on the good, the more good comes into my life.

I love myself, respect myself, and accept myself exactly as I am.

I am happy and at peace with myself.

Biblical Declarations

I am a princess of the most high God.

I am an heir to the royal kingdom.

I can do exceedingly abundantly above all that I can ask or think according to the power of God in me . . . to him be the Glory!

I have not been given a spirit of fear, but of power, love and a sound mind.

I am blessed in the city and in the country, going out and coming in.

I am the head and not the tail, above and not beneath — I shall lend to many nations and I shall not borrow.

I am anointed in the marketplace like Lydia, the seller of purple.

I am a woman of nobility and honor.

I find favor in the sight of God and man.

Everything I put my hand to prospers and succeeds.

I am a tree planted by the river of living water.

I trust in God with all my heart and I do not lean on my own understanding — in all my ways I acknowledge him and he will direct my paths.

I Am doing my best and God will bless it.

Angels open the storehouse of heaven to help me with my work.

I receive all the favor and abundance God has designed for me.

Quantum Physics, Beliefs, and Sound in the Bible

Mark 11:23
"For assuredly, I say to you, whoever says to this mountain, 'Be removed and be cast into the sea,' and does not doubt in his heart, but believes that those things he says will be done, he will have whatever he says."

Hebrews 11:1
"Now faith is the substance of things hoped for, the evidence of things not seen."

Romans 4:17

"As it is written: 'I have made you a father of many nations.' . . . before God whom he believed, the One giving life to the dead and calling into being the things not even existing."

Colossians 1:16-17

"For by him [Jesus] all things were created: things in heaven and on earth, visible and invisible, whether thrones or powers or rulers or authorities; all things were created by him and for him. He is before all things, and in him all things hold together."

Joshua 6:5

"It will be when they make a long blast with the ram's horn, when you hear the sound of the *shofar*, have all the people shout a loud shout — then the wall of the city will fall down flat, and the people will go up, everyone straight ahead."

John 20:26

"A week later his disciples were in the house again, and Thomas was with them. Though the doors were locked, Jesus came and stood among them and said, 'Peace be with you!' "

Mathew 8:13

"Then Jesus said to the Roman officer, 'Go back home. Because you believed, it has happened.' And the young servant was healed that same hour."

Romans 12:5

"We are many parts of one body, and we all belong to each other."

Proverbs 18:21

"Death and life are in the power of the tongue."

Deuteronomy 30:15

"Today I have given you the choice between life and death, between blessings and curses. Now I call on heaven and earth to witness the choice you make. Oh, that you would choose life, so that you and your descendants might live!"

Praise for RISE to Success and Patrice Lynn

"Patrice Lynn's masterwork **RISE to Success** is a must-read for anyone aspiring to change their current situation in life. Whether it is a desire for more money, a better job, or a loving relationship with a significant other; whatever it is, this book can help you achieve it. Patrice obviously knows what she is talking about. This book is well researched, and is laid out in a way that makes it easy to understand. The author also gives you a step-by-step plan for seamlessly implementing the books' strategies into your own life. I wish I had found a book like this 20 years ago when I first began my journey into the law of attraction and self-manifestation. It's like 15 books rolled onto one, and will save you many hours and days reading countless other books!"

— **Scott Henson**, President, Bumper Man Franchise

"I have read your book **RISE to Success**, and wow, what a gem. You have imagined, designed, and created a wonderfully rich, practicable, and lasting gift that will certainly inspire those who courageously RISE to their full potential! Fabulous writing, Patrice. I enjoyed the "you" in your book and all the great stories that bring your points to fruition. Very fun and informative, for sure."

— **Martha Hahn**, Chief, Science and Resource Management, Retired
Grand Canyon National Park

"Patrice, I like what you have done with **RISE to Success**. I believe it will help a lot of people."

— **Dr. Alexander Loyd**, PhD, ND
#1 Bestselling Author of *The Healing Code*

"Patrice projects that she believes in the innate goodness of all people and you in particular. She also inspires a sense of personal responsibility. She sees how much more effective people and businesses could be and seeks to help them get that way. I think her motivation is one of service more than having a job. She communicates well because she speaks form her heart as well as her mind. I wholeheartedly recommend Patrice."

— **Leslie Schultz**, Designer, Color World Printers

"**RISE to Success** came along at the perfect time in my life! Having a daily system to focus on my goals and visualize my ideal future gives me confidence that I will get results. The downloadable journals have been a huge benefit to me. **You have changed my life with these brain insights Patrice. Thank You.**"

— **Mark Hoover**, Real Estate Investor

"Patrice — lasting positive change & beauty are surely works of patience and persistence. You have helped me glimpse a "beauty way", a method and a habit of working life that can add up to quite a work of art. Thank You!"

— **David Adlai Adamson**, President, EcoBuild

"Patrice has written a powerful book, **RISE to Success**, that is a must-read for anyone interested in changing their habits. I've read other books in a similar vein — this one is the most cutting edge and relevant. The narrative is strong and to the point. Nothing is wasted. Change your life by reading this book."

— **Richard Campbell**, Co-author of *Writing Your Legacy: The Step-by-Step Guide to Crafting Your Life Story*

"Patrice, you have a great gift for expression and I can also see that you have a genuine concern for people. We are pleased to have you as an independent consultant and feel you will represent our philosophies of Principle-Centered Leadership very well."

— **Stephen R. Covey**, #1 Bestselling Author
The 7 Habits of Highly Effective People

"Each time our coaching session has ended I have felt like my head and heart have been expanded. Because of who you are — I grow. I expand. You encourage that in me."

— **Tom Jacobson**, IT Systems Manager, Healthcare

"Patrice Lynn is an extremely gifted and talented trainer. When I first saw Patrice present *The Accounting Game*, I realized she was one of those rare trainers that had the qualities I search for. She is very dynamic and can work with a group of people and keep several trains of thought going at one time. She knows how to connect with an audience with compassion and focus, and really knows how to have fun with people. People love Patrice and really open up in her presence."

— **Nancy Maresh**, Accelerated Learning Master
Founder, Brains At Work

"I have been in business for nearly fifteen years and have been very successful as a mail order vitamin and mineral company. Initially, I was not sure if I needed a consultant in light of my previous success. Was I wrong! Patrice's insightful advice and tireless support have motivated and inspired me and my team in ways that I couldn't foresee previously: the programs and structures she recommended and custom-tailored for my business are working. Our sales have increased and are on the up swing every month. I appreciate Patrice's expertise and I would not hesitate to recommend her for a start-up or successful business."

— **James Templeton**, President, Uni Key Health Systems

"I believe having Patrice as your coach is the right move. I have found her to be extremely valuable in several areas of Corporate Development. My work habits have improved immensely, especially my abilities to be more proactive, focused and organized. We are implementing an effective time management tool and I am aligning my weekly roles and goals with the bigger vision for my department. Patrice has helped me to clarify that vision, visualize my goals and begin to achieve them. The regular communication with her has begun to influence those around me. Patrice makes working with a coach a pleasure — her genuine concern comes through as well as her incredible wealth of knowledge. Patrice — thanks for the positive contribution you have made to my life!

— **Laura G. Malagon**, Quality Manager, Noven Pharmaceuticals

"As a top executive, it is challenging to balance all the demands on me. It is helpful to have Patrice to talk to — she helps me to stay focused on the factors critical to our success."

— **Robin Norris**, COO — Noven Pharmaceuticals

"I want to thank you for your dedicated and capable work over the past year as my executive coach. Your style is warm and accepting, but you expect effort from your clients, as you should. The positive impact of your help is already evident. I have expanded the business, added personnel, and take time for long-term planning. As you know, I've launched a major business venture, which converts one of my long-term goals into action. You have been both encouraging of this dream of mine, but you have also stressed the need for planning and identifying the critical success factors. With your tactful, but firm comments I now feel well grounded in the skills and the mental attitude necessary to make personal and business-related changes so I can be more organized and profitable."

— **Jon X. Giltner**, P.E. Engineer, JG&A Engineering Consultants

"Through her tough, but gentle approach, Patrice has empowered our 20-year old ADHD son to succeed in college. Since third grade we have been dragging him to counselors and specialists; he hated them all. When I told him about Patrice, he initially refused to meet her. Finally he agreed, but just for 1 or 2 sessions. That was a year ago; quickly he bonded with Patrice, and now he treasures his sessions with her. It's an expense, but the skills and strategies she gives him are priceless. Patrice is teaching our son to be a possibilities thinker, to set goals, and to stay focused."

— **Linda Vanderwold**, President, VanWrite Systems

"Patrice is an energetic, insightful Coach with a concrete understanding of the corporate and business world. At our first team meeting with Patrice we set a "Common Goal" of $16 million for the year with a net profit margin of 3.9%. Coaching has given me the confidence and tools to reach over $18 million in revenue, with a net profit of 7.2% — over $1,000,000! Patrice helped me to play to my strengths as a leader and assisted me in implementing several innovative business practices. We keep the lines of communication open with a "WIFLE" at the end of our weekly team meetings. Patrice also guided us in creating our industry niche and identifying the best companies to do business with, which brought increases in sales. The motivation she shared inspired us to go for an "Extreme Build" of the steel erection of a large retail store in 72 hours — a record! Patrice definitely adds value."

— **Shawn Brosam**, President, West Coast Iron

"You were one of the spiritual delights of our week together. I felt hum- bled, yet privileged to be entrusted with your story of growth, triumph and restored love. You are much more than a survivor — you are an "agent of transformation" for yourself and those around you. This gift will be multiplied many times over in your business. Thanks for being very special!"

— **Jim Rush**, Pastor and Counselor

"You have helped us accomplish so much in such a short period of time. You've been a real valuable friend, supporter and advisor to me and our *Outsourced CFO* practice. I would have never come up with the visual framework design you created on my own — it has been invaluable to bring a clear understanding of our program to our clients. Thank you for your wisdom, enthusiasm, and care for me and our firm."

— **Nate Riggan**, CPA, Founder, PointGuard Financial

"Anyone who desires an understanding of how to present information to others would benefit from attending Patrice Lynn's *"Learn Fast! The Art & Brain Science of Accelerated Learning."* This training gives a clear track on which to run providing experienced presenters the science behind what you already intuitively know, and inexperienced presenters a simple understanding of what to do to be successful. I was impressed with Patrice's humility and how much fun she had, which added so much to the training. I had fun — I am sure you will, too!"

— **Brian Bumpas**, Businessman, Real Estate

"I thought this would be another one of those events I was forced to attend, so I came prepared to sit in the back and work on other things. From the moment you opened your mouth I was totally, completely engaged and hung on your every word. Nice job!"

— **Daryl S. Paulsen**, CEO, Bioscience

"Patrice Lynn has the ability to take command of the room, unlike anyone I have ever seen. She is creative, engaging, hilarious!"

— **Dawn McGee**, CEO, Good Work Ventures

"Patrice lives what she teaches. She is an inspiring coach and her support and guidance is valuable. I have achieved clarity with regards to my goals and priorities. My focus and productivity has reached new heights."

— **H. Steve Ellenberg**, President Trumark Manufacturing

"Patrice worked with me at a crucial time of growth in our company. She was able to help me organize and concentrate my skill sets enabling me to become more productive, providing more time to focus on the big picture items. Our business increased profitability, margins, and was able to make major hiring moves in her wake. Never judgmental but always holding me accountable... her guidance helped me become more disciplined in my day to day routine and more successful in my business."

— **Loree Mulay Weisman**, President, CEO, Mulay's Sausage

"Patrice is truly one-of-a-kind. Mentoring under her many years ago proved to be absolutely pivotal in the course of my life. She was the spark that propelled me to success. She was a positive force in the universe then and I'm delighted to see that tradition continuing still today. Her presence makes the world a far better place; bring her into your own life, business or organization and you'll appreciate and understand my high recommendation."

— **Davey Lubin**, Owner, Captain, Naturalist, Esther G. Sea Taxi

"Patrice worked for Amway to develop a training system in a start-up manufacturing plant. Her knowledge and ability has led to a sustainable system that will ensure role-based curriculum and clear standard work. This type of work is very different than the traditional training environment. Patrice was able to learn quickly and adapt her skills to meet the business need."

— **Heather Scavo**, Six Sigma Black Belt, Amway

"Patrice brings together creativity, mindful-ness and intuition to create a powerful space for coaching. As my Mentor Coach, she helped me develop the presence and competence for the work i do today."

— **Sackeena Gordon Jones**, PhD, PCC, CTC, Executive Coach

About the Author

Patrice Lynn
"The Brain Training Expert"

On the front lines of personal and professional development, transformation and change for over 25 years, Patrice Lynn is a true veteran in her field. Patrice has had the privilege to assist thousands of business owners, teams, community leaders, entrepreneurs and individuals from all walks of life to become the best they can be.

Patrice Lynn is at her core, a teacher. A recognized training specialist, Patrice's ability to design engaging learning experiences sets her apart in her field. She is the gifted go-to expert who can make a significant difference in your events and large gatherings. Her consulting and training clients include large multi-national companies such as Patagonia, Hewlett Packard, Amway, The World Bank, and PricewaterhouseCoopers/PwC, as well as small and medium sized companies, and home-based businesses.

Her uncanny ability to see on many levels and bring forth the perfect nugget of wisdom opens clients to broader perspectives and breakthrough insights. Patrice is dedicated to help you cut through the mind clutter and empower you to refocus your life and business for optimum results.

On a never-ending quest to bring you the absolute best knowledge and tools, her certifications in training, coaching and personal transformation are top notch. A life, business, presentation, and ADHD coach since 1995. Patrice holds professional credentials with *The International Coach Federation, The*

Coaches Training Institute, ADD Coach Academy, and the *Barrett Values Center*'s *Cultural Transformation Tools*. At *ActionCOACH* she was a franchise owner and ranked in the top 10% of 1200 business coaches worldwide.

Patrice Lynn was one of the first five independent consultants certified to teach *The Seven Habits of Highly Effective People,* based on the book by Stephen R. Covey. She has personally met and learned from the greats in her field. A lifelong investment in business knowledge, training seminars, certifications, books, courses and conferences are available to you when you work with Patrice. Over 300 businesses and over 2,000 individuals have improved profits, performance, and achieved their dreams and goals.

No matter what Patrice did throughout her career, friends always asked if she was still doing *"that motivational speaking thing".* Her unique communication skills, combined with her edutainment style and sincere interest in people, are engaging. Her energy is infectious and she is a catalyst to inspire you to take action to achieve powerful results in your life. Follow her and together you will be on a fearless journey of adventure and exploration.

Today Patrice Lynn is at home in Sacramento, California. She enjoys the open-minded, friendly people who reside there, as well as the incredible natural beauty and mild Mediterranean climate. She loves the abundance of California's wineries and being by the water and the mountains. Patrice relishes holistic living, fitness, live music, worship, helping others, and sharing love and laughter with friends.

Visit www.patricelynn.com for FREE gifts, Products and Resources
Call 916-500-4206 to book Patrice to Speak
Or join her Group Coaching and Retreats